SPECTRUM

Test Prep

Grade 8

SPECTRUM

Columbus, Ohio

Credits:
School Specialty Publishing Editorial/Art & Design Team
Vincent F. Douglas, *President*
Tracey E. Dils, *Publisher*
Phyllis Sibbing, B.S. Ed., *Project Editor*
Rose Audette, *Art Director*

Also Thanks to:
MaryAnne Nestor, Layout and Production
Jenny Campbell, Interior Illustration

Send all inquiries to:
School Specialty Publishing
8720 Orion Place
Columbus, OH 43240-2111

ISBN 1-57768-668-3

8 9 10 11 12 13 POH 11 10 09 08 07 06

Table of Contents

About the Tests

What Are Standardized Achievement Tests?

Achievement tests measure what children know in particular subject areas such as reading, language arts, and mathematics. They do not measure your child's intelligence or ability to learn.

When tests are standardized, or *normed,* children's test results are compared with those of a specific group who have taken the test, usually at the same age or grade.

Standardized achievement tests measure what children around the country are learning. The test makers survey popular textbook series, as well as state curriculum frameworks and other professional sources, to determine what content is covered widely.

Because of variations in state frameworks and textbook series, as well as grade ranges on some test levels, the tests may cover some material that children have not yet learned. This is especially true if the test is offered early in the school year. However, test scores are compared to those of other children who take the test at the same time of year, so your child will not be at a disadvantage if his or her class has not covered specific material yet.

Different School Districts, Different Tests

There are many flexible options for districts when offering standardized tests. Many school districts choose not to give the full test battery, but select certain content and scoring options. For example, many schools may test only in the areas of reading and mathematics. Similarly, a state or district may use one test for certain grades and another test for other grades. These decisions are often based on the amount of time and money a district wishes to spend on test administration. Some states choose to develop their own statewide assessment tests.

On pages 5–7 you will find information about these five widely used standardized achievement tests:

- California Achievement Test (CAT)
- Terra Nova/CTBS
- Iowa Test of Basic Skills (ITBS)
- Stanford Achievement Test (SAT9)
- Metropolitan Achievement Test (MAT)

However, this book contains strategies and practice questions for use with a variety of tests. Even if your state does not give one of the five tests listed above, your child will benefit from doing the practice questions in this book. If you're unsure about which test your child takes, contact your local school district to find out which tests are given.

Types of Test Questions

Traditionally, standardized achievement tests have used only multiple choice questions. Today, many tests may include constructed response (short answer) and extended response (essay) questions as well.

In addition, many tests include questions that tap students' higher-order thinking skills. Instead of simple recall questions, such as identifying a date in history, questions may require students to make comparisons and contrasts, or analyze results, among other skills.

What the Tests Measure

These tests do not measure your child's level of intelligence, but they do show how well your child knows material that he or she has learned and that is also covered on the tests. It's important to remember that some tests cover content that is not taught in your child's school or grade. In other instances, depending on when in the year the test is given, your child may not yet have covered the material.

If the test reports you receive show that your child needs improvement in one or more skill areas, you may want to seek help from your child's teacher and find out how you can work with your child to improve his or her skills.

California Achievement Test (CAT/5)

What Is the *California Achievement Test*?

The *California Achievement Test* is a standardized achievement test battery that is widely used with elementary through high school students.

Parts of the Test

The *CAT* includes tests in the following content areas:

Reading
- Word Analysis
- Vocabulary
- Comprehension

Spelling

Language Arts
- Language Mechanics
- Language Usage

Mathematics

Science

Social Studies

Your child may take some or all of these subtests if your district uses the *California Achievement Test*.

Terra Nova/CTBS (Comprehensive Tests of Basic Skills)

What Is the *Terra Nova/CTBS*?

The *Terra Nova/Comprehensive Tests of Basic Skills* is a standardized achievement test battery used in elementary through high school grades.

While many of the test questions on the *Terra Nova* are in the traditional multiple choice form, your child may take parts of the *Terra Nova* that include some open-ended questions (constructed-response items).

Parts of the Test

Your child may take some or all of the following subtests if your district uses the *Terra Nova/CTBS*:

Reading/Language Arts
Mathematics
Science
Social Studies
Supplementary tests include:
- Word Analysis
- Vocabulary
- Language Mechanics
- Spelling
- Mathematics Computation

Critical thinking skills may also be tested.

Iowa Test of Basic Skills (ITBS)

What Is the *ITBS*?

The *Iowa Test of Basic Skills* is a standardized achievement test battery used in elementary through high school grades.

Parts of the Test

Your child may take some or all of these subtests if your district uses the *ITBS*, also known as the *Iowa*:

Reading
- Vocabulary
- Reading Comprehension

Language Arts
- Spelling
- Capitalization
- Punctuation
- Usage and Expression

Mathematics
- Concepts/Estimate
- Problems/Data Interpretation

Social Studies
Science
Sources of Information

Stanford Achievement Test (SAT9)

What Is the *Stanford Achievement Test*?

The *Stanford Achievement Test, Ninth Edition (SAT9)* is a standardized achievement test battery used in elementary through high school grades.

Note that the *Stanford Achievement Test (SAT9)* is a different test from the *SAT* used by high school students for college admissions.

While many of the test questions on the *SAT9* are in traditional multiple choice form, your child may take parts of the *SAT9* that include some open-ended questions (constructed-response items).

Parts of the Test

Your child may take some or all of these subtests if your district uses the *Stanford Achievement Test:*

Reading
- Vocabulary
- Reading Comprehension

Mathematics
- Problem Solving
- Procedures

Language Arts
Spelling
Study Skills
Listening

Critical thinking skills may also be tested.

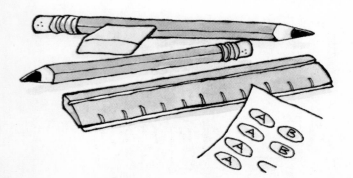

Metropolitan Achievement Test (MAT7 and MAT8)

What Is the *Metropolitan Achievement Test*?

The *Metropolitan Achievement Test* is a standardized achievement test battery used in elementary through high school grades.

Parts of the Test

Your child may take some or all of these subtests if your district uses the *Metropolitan Achievement Test:*

Reading
- Vocabulary
- Reading Comprehension

Mathematics
- Concepts and Problem Solving
- Computation

Language Arts
- Pre-writing
- Composing
- Editing

Science
Social Studies
Research Skills
Thinking Skills
Spelling

Statewide Assessments

Today the majority of states give statewide assessments. In some cases these tests are known as *high-stakes assessments*. This means that students must score at a certain level in order to be promoted. Some states use minimum competency or proficiency tests. Often these tests measure more basic skills than other types of statewide assessments.

Statewide assessments are generally linked to state curriculum frameworks. Frameworks provide a blueprint, or outline, to ensure that teachers are covering the same curriculum topics as other teachers in the same grade level in the state. In some states, standardized achievement tests (such as the five described in this book) are used in connection with statewide assessments.

When Statewide Assessments Are Given

Statewide assessments may not be given at every grade level. Generally, they are offered at one or more grades in elementary school, middle school, and high school. Many states test at grades 4, 8, and 10.

State-by-State Information

You can find information about statewide assessments and curriculum frameworks at your state Department of Education Web site. To find the address for your individual state, go to www.ed.gov, click on Topics A–Z, and then click on State Departments of Education. You will find a list of all the state departments of education, mailing addresses, and Web sites.

How to Help Your Child Prepare for Standardized Testing

Preparing All Year Round

Perhaps the most valuable way you can help your child prepare for standardized achievement tests is by providing enriching experiences. Keep in mind also that test results for younger children are not as reliable as for older students. If a child is hungry, tired, or upset, this may result in a poor test score. Here are some tips on how you can help your child do his or her best on standardized tests.

Read aloud with your child. Reading aloud helps develop vocabulary and fosters a positive attitude toward reading. Reading together is one of the most effective ways you can help your child succeed in school.

Share experiences. Baking cookies together, planting a garden, or making a map of your neighborhood are examples of activities that help build skills that are measured on the tests, such as sequencing and following directions.

Become informed about your state's testing procedures. Ask about or watch for announcements of meetings that explain about standardized tests and statewide assessments in your school district. Talk to your child's teacher about your child's individual performance on these state tests during a parent-teacher conference.

Help your child know what to expect. Read and discuss with your child the test-taking tips in this book. Your child can prepare by working through a couple of strategies a day so that no practice session takes too long.

Help your child with his or her regular school assignments. Set up a quiet study area for homework. Supply this area with pencils, paper, markers, a calculator, a ruler, a dictionary, scissors, glue, and so on. Check your child's homework and offer to help if he or she gets stuck. But remember, it's your child's homework, not yours. If you help too much, your child will not benefit from the activity.

Keep in regular contact with your child's teacher. Attend parent-teacher conferences, school functions, PTA or PTO meetings, and school board meetings. This will help you get to know the educators in your district and the families of your child's classmates.

Learn to use computers as an educational resource. If you do not have a computer and Internet access at home, try your local library.

Remember—simply getting your child comfortable with testing procedures and helping him or her know what to expect can improve test scores!

Getting Ready for the Big Day

There are lots of things you can do on or immediately before test day to improve your child's chances of testing success. What's more, these strategies will help your child prepare him– or herself for school tests, too, and promote general study skills that can last a lifetime.

Provide a good breakfast on test day.
Instead of sugar cereal, which provides immediate but not long-term energy, have your child eat a breakfast with protein or complex carbohydrates, such as an egg, whole grain cereal or toast, or a banana-yogurt shake.

Promote a good night's sleep. A good night's sleep before the test is essential. Try not to overstress the importance of the test. This may cause your child to lose sleep because of anxiety. Doing some exercise after school and having a quiet evening routine will help your child sleep well the night before the test.

Assure your child that he or she is not expected to know all of the answers on the test. Explain that other children in higher grades may take the same test, and that the test may measure things your child has not yet learned in school. Help your child understand that you expect him or her to put forth a good effort—and that this is enough. Your child should not try to cram for these tests. Also avoid threats or bribes; these put undue pressure on children and may interfere with their best performance.

Keep the mood light and offer encouragement. To provide a break on test days, do something fun and special after school— take a walk around the neighborhood, play a game, read a favorite book, or prepare a special snack together. These activities keep your child's mood light—even if the testing sessions have been difficult—and show how much you appreciate your child's effort.

Taking Standardized Tests

No matter what grade you're in, this is information you can use to prepare for standardized tests. Here is what you'll find:

- Test-taking tips and strategies to use on test day and year round.
- Important terms to know for Language Arts, Reading, Math, Science, and Social Studies.
- A checklist of skills to complete to help you understand what you need to know in Language Arts, Reading Comprehension, Writing, and Math.
- General study/homework tips.

By opening this book, you've already taken your first step towards test success. The rest is easy—all you have to do is get started!

What You Need to Know

There are many things you can do to increase your test success. Here's a list of tips to keep in mind when you take standardized tests—and when you study for them, too.

Keep up with your school work. One way you can succeed in school and on tests is by studying and doing your homework regularly. Studies show that you remember only about one-fifth of what you memorize the night before a test. That's one good reason not to try to learn it all at once! Keeping up with your work throughout the year will help you remember the material better. You also won't be as tired or nervous as if you try to learn everything at once.

Feel your best. One of the ways you can do your best on tests and in school is to make sure your body is ready. To do this, get a good night's sleep each night and eat a healthy breakfast (not sugary cereal that will leave you tired by the middle of the morning). An egg or a milkshake with yogurt and fresh fruit will give you lasting energy. Also, wear comfortable clothes, maybe your lucky shirt or your favorite color on test day. It can't hurt, and it may even help you relax.

Be prepared. Do practice questions and learn about how standardized tests are organized. Books like this one will help you know what to expect when you take a standardized test.

When you are taking the test, follow the directions. It is important to listen carefully to the directions your teacher gives and to read the written instructions carefully. Words like *not*, *none*, *rarely*, *never*, and *always* are very important in test directions and questions. You may want to circle words like these.

Look at each page carefully before you start answering. In school you usually read a passage and then answer questions about it. But when you take a test, it's helpful to follow a different order.

If you are taking a Reading test, first read the directions. Then read the *questions* before you read the passage. This way, you will know exactly what kind of information to look for as you read. Next, read the passage carefully. Finally, answer the questions.

On math and science tests, look at the labels on graphs and charts. Think about what each graph or chart shows. Questions often will ask you to draw conclusions about the information.

Manage your time. *Time management* means using your time wisely on a test so that you can finish as much of it as possible and do your best. Look over the test or the parts that you are allowed to do at one time. Sometimes you may want to do the easier parts first. This way, if you run out of time before you finish, you will have completed a good chunk of the work.

For tests that have a time limit, notice what time it is when the test begins and figure out when you need to stop. Check a few times as you work through the test to be sure you are making good progress and not spending too much time on any particular section.

You don't have to keep up with everyone else. You may notice other students in the class finishing before you do. Don't worry about this. Everyone works at a different pace. Just keep going, trying not to spend too long on any one question.

Fill in answer circles properly. Even if you know every answer on a test, you won't do well unless you enter the answers correctly on the answer sheet.

Fill in the entire circle, but don't spend too much time making it perfect. Make your mark dark, but not so dark that it goes through the paper! And be sure you choose only one answer for each question, even if you are not sure. If you choose two answers, both will be marked as wrong.

It's usually not a good idea to change your answers. Usually your first choice is the right one. Unless you realize that you misread the question, the directions, or some facts in a passage, it's usually safer to stay with your first answer. If you are pretty sure it's wrong, of course, go ahead and change it. Make sure you completely erase the first choice and neatly fill in your new choice.

Use context clues to figure out tough questions. If you come across a word or idea you don't understand, use context clues—the words in the sentences nearby—to help you figure out its meaning.

Sometimes it's good to guess. Should you guess when you don't know an answer on a test? That depends. If your teacher has made the test, usually you will score better if you answer as many questions as possible, even if you don't really know the answers.

On standardized tests, here's what to do to score your best. For each question, most of these tests let you choose from four or five answer choices. If you decide that a couple of answers are clearly wrong, but you're still not sure about the answer, go ahead and make your best guess. If you can't narrow down the choices at all, then you may be better off skipping the question. Tests like these take away extra points for wrong answers, so it's better to leave them blank. Be sure you skip over the answer space for these questions on the answer sheet, though, so you don't fill in the wrong spaces.

Sometimes you should skip a question and come back to it. On many tests, you will score better if you answer more questions. This means that you should not spend too much time on any single question. Sometimes it gets tricky, though, keeping track of questions you skipped on your answer sheet.

If you want to skip a question because you don't know the answer, put a very light pencil mark next to the question in the test booklet. Try to choose an answer, even if you're not sure of it. Fill in the answer lightly on the answer sheet.

Check your work. On a standardized test, you can't go ahead or skip back to another section of the test. But you may go back and review your answers on the section you just worked on if you have extra time.

First, scan your answer sheet. Make sure that you answered every question you could. Also, if you are using a bubble-type answer sheet, make sure that you filled in only one bubble for each question. Erase any extra marks on the page.

Finally—avoid test anxiety! If you get nervous about tests, don't worry. *Test anxiety* happens to lots of good students. Being a little nervous actually sharpens your mind. But if you get very nervous about tests, take a few minutes to relax the night before or the day of the test. One good way to relax is to get some exercise, even if you just have time to stretch, shake out your fingers, and wiggle your toes. If you can't move around, it helps just to take a few slow, deep breaths and picture yourself doing a great job!

Terms to Know

Here's a list of terms that are good to know when taking standardized tests. Don't be worried if you see something new. You may not have learned it in school yet.

acute angle   an angle of less than 90 degrees

area   the amount of surface within a flat shape

asteroid   a tiny planet which orbits the sun

atom   the smallest part of an element that still has all the properties of that element

atomic weight   the average weight of one atom of an element

boiling point   the temperature at which a liquid boils

cell   the smallest unit of an organism capable of functioning on its own; most have a cell membrane, cytoplasm, other organs, and at least one nucleus

chemical change   a permanent change to a substance which affects the chemical composition of that substance

circumference   the distance around a circle

comet   an object, often brightly lit, which has a long tail of light and travels around the sun

congruent   equal in size or shape

delta   a triangle-shaped area of land where sand or mud collects from a river entering the sea

diameter   the distance across a circle at its widest point

electron   a negatively charged particle which moves around the nucleus of an atom

element   a substance which cannot be broken down into other substances

equator   the imaginary line that divides the Earth in half, exactly between the North and South poles

exponent   a number that shows how many times another number is to be multiplied by itself; usually placed to the right and above that number

factor   a whole number that can be divided into a larger number without remainder

freezing point   the temperature at which a specific liquid turns to a solid

integer   any whole number, positive or negative

latitude   the location of a specific place, measured in degrees north or south of the equator

longitude   the location of a specific place, measured in degrees east or west of the prime meridian

melting point   the temperature at which a specific solid, when heated, becomes a liquid

metaphor   a method of describing one thing by calling it something else

neutron   a type of particle found within the nucleus of an atom; it usually has no charge

obtuse angle   an angle larger than 90 degrees but less than 180 degrees

parallel   two straight lines are said to be parallel if they are the same distance from one another at every point and never meet

peninsula   a land form that juts out from a larger body of land and is almost entirely surrounded by water

perimeter   the distance around a shape or object

perpendicular   a line that creates right angles when it intersects with another line

physical change   a reversible change to a substance in which the chemical composition of that substance stays the same

polygon   a flat shape with at least three straight sides

predicate   the part of a sentence that tells what the subject did or was done to the subject

prefix   a group of letters added to the beginning of a word or root to change its meaning

prime meridian   the imaginary line of longitude, passing through Greenwich, England, from which all other longitude is measured

prime number   a number with exactly two factors

probability   the likelihood that an event will happen

proton   a type of particle found within the nucleus of an atom; usually positively charged

quotient   the number that results from dividing one number by another

radius   the distance from the center of a circle to any point along its outer edge

ratio   a comparison of two numbers or quantities, usually expressed as a fraction

ray   a piece of a line that starts at a given point and extends infinitely in one direction

right angle   an angle of exactly 90 degrees

satellite   a heavenly body that orbits another heavenly body

segment   a part of a line with a definite ending and starting point

simile   a description that tells about one thing by comparing it to something else

square root   the factor of a number which, when multiplied by itself, results in that number

suffix   a group of letters added to the end of a word or root to change its meaning

volume   the amount of space within a three-dimensional (solid) shape

Skills Checklist

Which subjects do you need more practice in? Use the following checklist to find out. Put a check mark next to each statement that is true for you. Then use the unchecked statements to figure out which skills you need to review.

Keep in mind that if you are using the checklist in the middle of the school year, you may not have learned some skills yet. Talk to your teacher or a parent if you need help with a new skill.

Reading

☐ I can use context clues to figure out tough words.

☐ I know what synonyms are and how to use them.

☐ I know what antonyms are and how to use them.

☐ I can find words with opposite meanings.

☐ I can tell the difference between a fact and an opinion.

☐ I know the different genres of writing (fiction, nonfiction, etc.)

☐ I can predict what will happen next in a story.

☐ I can paraphrase and summarize what I read.

☐ I can compare and contrast characters and events.

☐ I can rephrase the main idea in a sentence or paragraph.

☐ I can recognize the author's purpose for writing.

☐ I can choose the correct topic sentence for a paragraph.

Language Arts

I can identify the different parts of speech.

☐ subject and object pronouns

☐ direct and indirect objects

☐ prepositions

☐ verbs

☐ verb tenses (past, present, and future)

☐ linking verbs

☐ adjectives

☐ adverbs

☐ conjunctions

☐ prefixes and suffixes

Do your homework right away. Set aside a special time every day after school to do your homework. You may want to take a break when you first get home, but give yourself plenty of time to do your homework, too. That way, you won't get interrupted by dinner or get too tired to finish.

If you are bored or confused by an assignment and you really don't want to do it, promise yourself a little reward, perhaps a snack or 15 minutes of playing ball after you've really worked hard for 45 minutes or so. Then go back to work for a while if you need to, and take another break later.

Get help if you need it. If you need help, just ask. Call a friend or ask a family member for help. If these people can't help you, be sure to ask your teacher the next day about any work you didn't understand.

Use a computer. If you have one available, a computer can be a great tool for doing homework. Typing your homework on the computer lets you hand in neat papers, check your spelling easily, and look up the definitions of words you aren't sure about. If you have an Internet connection, you can also do research without leaving home.

Before you go online, talk with your family about ways to stay safe. Be sure never to give out personal information (your name, age, address, or phone number) without permission.

Practice, practice, practice! The best way to improve your skills in specific subject areas is through lots of practice. If you have trouble in a school subject such as math, science, social studies, language arts, or reading, doing some extra activities or projects can give you just the boost you need.

Homework Log
and Weekly Schedule

	Monday	Tuesday	Wednesday
MATH			
SOCIAL STUDIES			
SCIENCE			
READING			
LANGUAGE ARTS			
OTHER			

for the week of _____

	Thursday	Friday	Saturday / Sunday	
				MATH
				SOCIAL STUDIES
				SCIENCE
				READING
				LANGUAGE ARTS
				OTHER

What's Ahead in This Book?

As you know, you will have to take many tests while in school. But there is no reason to be nervous about taking standardized tests. You can prepare for them by doing your best in school all year. You can also learn about the types of questions you'll see on standardized tests and helpful strategies for answering the questions. That's what this book is all about. It has been developed especially to help you and other eighth graders know what to expect—and what to do—on test day.

The first section will introduce you to the different kinds of questions found on most standardized tests. Multiple choice, short answer, matching, and other types of questions will be explained in detail. You'll get tips for answering each type. Then you'll be given sample questions to work through so you can practice your skills.

Next, you'll find sections on these major school subjects: reading, language arts, math, social studies (sometimes called citizenship), and science. You'll discover traps to watch for in each subject area and tricks you can use to make answering the questions easier. And there are plenty of practice questions provided to sharpen your skills even more.

Finally, you'll find two sections of questions. One is called Practice Test and the other is called Final Test. The questions are designed to look just like the ones you'll be given in school on a real standardized test. An answer key is at the back of the book so you can check your own answers. Once you check your answers, you can see in which subject areas you need more practice.

So good luck—test success is just around the corner!

Multiple Choice Questions

You have probably seen multiple choice questions before. They are the most common type of question used on standardized tests. To answer a multiple choice question, you must choose one answer from a number of choices.

EXAMPLE   **Which word does not fit in this group?**
salmon, trout, _____

  Ⓐ tuna

  Ⓑ swordfish

  Ⓒ shark

  Ⓓ dolphin

Sometimes you will know the answer right away. Other times you won't. To answer multiple choice questions, do the following:

- Read the directions carefully. If you're not sure what you're supposed to do, you might make a lot of mistakes.
- First answer any easy questions whose answers you are *sure* you know.
- When you come to a harder question, circle the question number. You can come back to this question after you have finished all the easier ones.
- Watch out for clue words like *same, opposite, not, probably, best, most likely,* and *main.* They can change the meaning of a question and/or help you eliminate answer choices.

Remember

Words like *same, opposite, not, probably, best, main,* and *most likely,* can change the meaning of a question.

Testing It Out

Now look at the sample question more closely.

Think: Let's see: salmon and trout are fish. I see the word *not,* so I'm looking for a word that is *not* another fish name. Tuna and swordfish are both fish, so **A** and **B** are wrong. I'm not sure if a shark is a fish, but I do know that a dolphin is an aquatic mammal—not a fish—so I will choose **D**.

Multiple Choice Practice

Directions: Answer questions 1–4.

Directions: Read the following passage. Then answer the questions below.

1   **Forthright is an antonym for _____.**

Ⓐ stealthy

Ⓑ sincere

Ⓒ honest

Ⓓ genuine

2   **Gruesome is a synonym for _____.**

Ⓕ beautiful

Ⓖ exquisite

Ⓗ ghastly

Ⓙ sublime

3   **Which word fits best in this group?**

mystery, comedy, _____

Ⓐ sleuth

Ⓑ movie

Ⓒ romance

Ⓓ detective

4   **Which word could not fit in this group?**

gabby, talkative, _____

Ⓕ chatty

Ⓖ loose-lipped

Ⓗ garrulous

Ⓙ mute

The Mayans occupied the region that is now southern Mexico, Belize, Guatemala, and Honduras. Scientists believe they moved down the Pacific coast in waves, reaching southern Mexico by about 5000 BC. At first, they lived in simple communities that depended on fishing and gathering fruits, vegetables, and grains. They gradually moved inland, and by 2000 BC or earlier, learned how to grow crops. They cultivated a variety of foods, including beans, squash, tomatoes, peppers, and different fruit. Their chief food was maize, a type of corn.

5   **What is the meaning of the word *waves*?**

Ⓐ boats

Ⓑ ocean

Ⓒ stages

Ⓓ groups

6   **What allowed the ancient Mayans to move away from the coastline?**

Ⓕ building planned cities

Ⓖ creating a calendar

Ⓗ discovering a new river

Ⓙ learning how to grow crops

Fill-in-the-Blank Questions

On some tests you must fill in something that's missing from a phrase, sentence, equation, or passage.

EXAMPLE   **You will have to complete this form to _____ for the job.**

    Ⓐ waiter   Ⓒ interview

    Ⓑ apply   Ⓓ astute

To answer fill-in-the-blank questions, do the following:

- See if you can think of the answer even before you look at your choices.
- Even if the answer you first thought of is one of the choices, be sure to check the other choices. There may be a better answer.
- Look for the articles *a* and *an* before the blank. The word *a* must be followed by a consonant and *an* is followed by words starting with vowel sounds.
- For harder questions, try to fit every answer choice into the blank. Write an X after answers that do not fit. Choose the answer that does fit.
- If you get really stuck, try filling in the blank on your own (not choosing from the given answers). Then look for synonyms for your new word/words among the answer choices.

Testing It Out

Now look at the sample question above more closely.

Think: Choice A, *waiter*, is a type of job. That answer doesn't make any sense in this sentence.

Choice **B**, *apply*, makes complete sense. "You will have to complete this form to *apply* for the job." This is probably the answer, but I'll double-check the others to make sure.

Interview, choice **C**, is also a possibility. "You will have to complete this form to *interview* for the job." That could mean something like "You will have to fill out a form in order to talk to someone about the job."

Choice **D**, *astute*, means "clever." That choice makes no sense.

So back to choices **B** and **C**; although *interview* might fit in the sentence, *apply* fits better. So the answer must be **B**, *apply*.

Fill-in-the-Blank Practice

Directions: Find the word that best completes each sentence.

1 Mei and I _____ to spend the summer backpacking across Europe.

 Ⓐ revolved   Ⓒ fluctuated

 Ⓑ resolved   Ⓓ remembered

2 We slept in hostels and cooked our meals in _____ kitchens.

 Ⓕ capricious   Ⓗ communal

 Ⓖ coexist   Ⓙ company

3 Mei's guidebook had _____ descriptions of famous attractions.

 Ⓐ succinct   Ⓒ blatant

 Ⓑ compatible   Ⓓ curt

4 We got lost, arriving at Blackheath Castle by a _____ route.

 Ⓕ direct   Ⓗ picturesque

 Ⓖ linear   Ⓙ roundabout

5 An _____ guide, familiar with the history of the castle, gave us a tour.

 Ⓐ shallow   Ⓒ short

 Ⓑ intelligent   Ⓓ inept

6 I was _____ by the intricate stone carvings on the castle's walls.

 Ⓕ enthralled   Ⓗ bored

 Ⓖ embarrassed   Ⓙ happy

7 In the castle's gardens, we found a _____ made out of hedges.

 Ⓐ labyrinth   Ⓒ moat

 Ⓑ cardinal   Ⓓ tangle

8 When we got hungry, we _____ Mei's guidebook to find a place to eat.

 Ⓕ remembered   Ⓗ ignored

 Ⓖ consulted   Ⓙ contrived

9 The guidebook _____ a small restaurant on the main street.

 Ⓐ told   Ⓒ recommended

 Ⓑ recognized   Ⓓ choose

10 At the restaurant we had a _____ feast—fit for a king!

 Ⓕ expensive

 Ⓖ terrible

 Ⓗ poisonous

 Ⓙ sumptuous

True/False Questions

A true/false question asks you to read a statement and decide if it is right (true) or wrong (false). Sometimes you will be asked to write **T** for true or **F** for false. Most of the time you must fill in a circle for your answer.

EXAMPLE   **Marie Curie, Leonardo da Vinci, and William Shakespeare are all famous scientists.**

   Ⓐ   true

   Ⓑ   false

To answer true/false questions, do the following:

• First, answer all of the easy questions. Circle the numbers next to harder ones and come back to them later.
• True/false questions with words like *always*, *never*, *all*, *none*, *only* and *every* are usually false. This is because they limit a statement so much.
• True/false questions with words like *most*, *many*, and *generally* are often true. This is because they make statements more believable.
• Remember that if any part of a statement is false, the entire statement is false.

 **Remember**

True/false questions with words like *always, never, all, none, only,* and *every* are usually false.

Testing It Out

Now look at the sample question more closely.

 Think: I know that Marie Curie won the Nobel Prize in Physics and Chemistry. She was definitely a famous scientist. Leonardo da Vinci painted *The Mona Lisa*. He was a famous artist, but I'm not sure if he was a scientist, too. But I know that William Shakespeare was an author. So the answer must be **B** for false.

True/False Practice

Directions: Read the passage. Then decide if each statement is true or false.

Leonardo da Vinci believed in *saper vedere*, or the power of observation. While his contemporaries looked for scientific truth in the writings of the ancient scholars, da Vinci's theories were based on empirical research, that which he observed and recorded in his many notebooks.

"How does the human body work?" da Vinci asked himself. To answer this question, da Vinci learned to dissect cadavers—usually the bodies of dead criminals. He then made thousands of detailed sketches of their muscles, organs, and skeletons.

1 *Saper vedere* and the power of observation most likely mean the same thing.

Ⓐ true
Ⓑ false

2 Empirical research is based on observations.

Ⓐ true
Ⓑ false

3 To learn about the human body, da Vinci only read books.

Ⓐ true
Ⓑ false

4 The word cadaver and the word criminal mean the same thing.

Ⓐ true
Ⓑ false

5 da Vinci probably made sketches of the heart.

Ⓐ true
Ⓑ false

6 In the context of the passage above, the word empirical means minor.

Ⓐ true
Ⓑ false

7 da Vinci conducted his research exactly like other Renaissance scientists.

Ⓐ true
Ⓑ false

8 Today we know how the human body's muscles work thanks to da Vinci's research.

Ⓐ true
Ⓑ false

Matching Questions

Matching questions ask you to find pairs of words or phrases that are related in a certain way. You may be asked to draw lines or fill in circles to show your answers.

EXAMPLE **Match items that go together.**

1	engineer	A	microscope	1	Ⓐ Ⓑ Ⓒ Ⓓ
2	musician	B	calculator	2	Ⓐ Ⓑ Ⓒ Ⓓ
3	botanist	C	turntable	3	Ⓐ Ⓑ Ⓒ Ⓓ
4	deejay	D	cello	4	Ⓐ Ⓑ Ⓒ Ⓓ

When answering matching questions, follow these simple guidelines:

- Begin by figuring out the relationship between the two groups of words.
- When you first look at a matching question, you will probably be able to spot some of the matches right away. So match the easiest choices first.
- If you come to a word you don't know, look for prefixes, suffixes, or root words to help figure out its meaning.
- Some matching items contain phrases rather than single words. Begin with the column that has the most words. This column will usually give the most information.
- Work down one column at a time. It is confusing to switch back and forth.

Testing It Out

Now look at the sample questions more closely.

 Think: The first column is a list of careers, and the second column shows tools that people use to help them do their work.

An *engineer* uses a *calculator*, so I see that the answer to number 1 is choice **B**.

A *musician* could play any number of musical instruments. I see that choice **D** is *cello*, which is a type of musical instrument, so the answer to number 2 is **D**.

A *botanist* is some sort of scientist. I'm not exactly sure what they study. But I know that many scientists use microscopes. So logically, **A** is the correct answer.

The last word in the first column is *deejay*. The only remaining choice in the second column is *turntable*, which is definitely something a *deejay* would use. So the answer to number 4 is **C**.

Matching Practice

Directions: For numbers 1–16, match words or phrases that go together.

1	×	A 7	**1**	Ⓐ Ⓑ Ⓒ Ⓓ
2	3 + ⁻2 + ⁻5	B	**2**	Ⓐ Ⓑ Ⓒ Ⓓ
3	(3 + 8 ×4) ÷ 5	C ⁻4	**3**	Ⓐ Ⓑ Ⓒ Ⓓ
4	4 ×(8 – 5)	D 12	**4**	Ⓐ Ⓑ Ⓒ Ⓓ

5	Emily Dickenson	F self-taught painter	**5**	Ⓕ Ⓖ Ⓗ Ⓙ
6	Lilioukalani	G founder of the Red Cross	**6**	Ⓕ Ⓖ Ⓗ Ⓙ
7	Grandma Moses	H the last Queen of Hawaii	**7**	Ⓕ Ⓖ Ⓗ Ⓙ
8	Clara Barton	J poet	**8**	Ⓕ Ⓖ Ⓗ Ⓙ

9	Rhode Island	A Juneau	**9**	Ⓐ Ⓑ Ⓒ Ⓓ
10	Alaska	B Albany	**10**	Ⓐ Ⓑ Ⓒ Ⓓ
11	Virginia	C Richmond	**11**	Ⓐ Ⓑ Ⓒ Ⓓ
12	New York	D Providence	**12**	Ⓐ Ⓑ Ⓒ Ⓓ

13	meter	F milk	**13**	Ⓕ Ⓖ Ⓗ Ⓙ
14	kilometers	G caterpillar	**14**	Ⓕ Ⓖ Ⓗ Ⓙ
15	centimeters	H cloth	**15**	Ⓕ Ⓖ Ⓗ Ⓙ
16	liter	J marathon	**16**	Ⓕ Ⓖ Ⓗ Ⓙ

Directions: For numbers 17–20, match words with opposite meanings.

17	force	A kindness	**17**	Ⓐ Ⓑ Ⓒ Ⓓ
18	spite	B argument	**18**	Ⓐ Ⓑ Ⓒ Ⓓ
19	agreement	C persuade	**19**	Ⓐ Ⓑ Ⓒ Ⓓ
20	ephemeral	D enduring	**20**	Ⓐ Ⓑ Ⓒ Ⓓ

Analogy Questions

In an analogy question, you must figure out the relationship between two things. Then you must complete another pair with the same relationship.

EXAMPLE   <u>Rule by a few</u> is to <u>oligarchy</u> as <u>rule by a queen</u> is to _____.

    Ⓐ democracy   Ⓒ monarchy

    Ⓑ theocracy   Ⓓ monopoly

Analogies usually have two pairs of items. In this question, the two pairs are *rule by a few/oligarchy* and *rule by a queen/_____*. To answer analogy questions, do the following:

- Find the missing item that completes the second pair. To do this, figure out how the first pair of items relate to each other. Form a sentence that explains how they are related.
- Next, use your sentence to figure out the missing word in the second pair of items.
- For more difficult analogies, try each answer choice in the sentence you formed. Choose the answer that fits best.
- Think about whether you are looking for a noun, verb, adjective, or other part of speech

Testing It Out

Now look at the sample question more closely.

Think: I'll make a sentence out of the first pair: "If a country is ruled by a few, it is called an *oligarchy*." The new sentence I need to complete is "When a country is ruled by a queen, it is called a _____."

"When a country is ruled by a queen, it is called a *democracy*." Choice **A** isn't correct.

Choice **B** would be "When a country is ruled by a queen, it is called a *theocracy*." I'm not sure what the word *theocracy* means. So I'll skip this choice for now, and come back to it if I can't find a better choice.

If I insert choice **C** into my sentence, I get "When a country is ruled by a queen, it is called a *monarchy*." That's true. **C** is a good choice.

D would be "When a country is ruled by a queen, it is called a *monopoly*." The word *monopoly* describes a business, not a government. So **D** is probably not the correct answer.

I'll choose **C**, *monarchy*, as my answer.

Analogy Practice

Directions: Find the word that best completes each analogy.

1 Lava is to volcano as stalactite is to _____.

Ⓐ moon
Ⓑ ocean
Ⓒ island
Ⓓ cave

2 Diminutive is to colossal as trepidation is to _____.

Ⓕ cowardice
Ⓖ brave
Ⓗ consternation
Ⓙ mettle

3 Declaration of war is to abhorrence as peace agreement is to _____.

Ⓐ amity
Ⓑ hatred
Ⓒ liberation
Ⓓ discord

4 Moldy is to rancid as edict is to _____.

Ⓕ eviction
Ⓖ proclamation
Ⓗ conviction
Ⓙ cheese

5 Meteor is to astronomer as geode is to _____.

Ⓐ geographer
Ⓑ archeologist
Ⓒ anthropologist
Ⓓ geologist

6 World Wide Web is to www as self-contained underwater breathing apparatus is to _____.

Ⓕ SCUBA
Ⓖ NASA
Ⓗ HTML
Ⓙ SCAB

7 Stomach is to digestion as lung is to _____.

Ⓐ transpiration
Ⓑ respiration
Ⓒ dehydration
Ⓓ circulation

8 Author is to dissertation as composer is to _____.

Ⓕ orchestra
Ⓖ fortissimo
Ⓗ symphonic
Ⓙ concerto

Short Answer Questions

Some test questions don't give you answers to choose from. Instead, you must write short answers in your own words. They often ask you to respond to a passage or other information you have been given. These are called "short answer" or "open response" questions.

EXAMPLE

Over the past several hundred years, zoos have changed considerably. At first, they were no better than prisons for animals, with small cages and barely acceptable food. In the last fifty or so years, however, zoos have provided animals with larger and more natural habitats, better food, and opportunities for recreation and socialization. Zoos also moved from being purely entertainment to serving as research and education centers. These changes have improved life for the animals in the zoos.

Do you think that modern zoos are better than the zoos that existed several hundred years ago? Why? _____

When you write short answers to questions, do the following:

- Read each question carefully. Make sure to respond directly to the question that is being asked, not to details or statements that are given elsewhere in the body of the question.
- Your response should be short but complete. On one hand, you don't want to waste time including unnecessary information in your answer. On the other hand, make sure to answer the entire question, not just a part of it.
- Write in complete sentences unless the directions say you don't have to.
- Make sure to double-check your answers for spelling, punctuation, and grammar.

Testing It Out

Now look at the sample question more closely.

Think: Zoos have changed for the better in the past several centuries. So I will write:

I think that zoos are better now. In a modern zoo, animals have adequate space to exercise, the opportunity to interact with other animals, better food, and caretakers who know a great deal about animals.

Short Answer Practice

Directions: Read the passage below. Then answer the questions.

In the mid-1930s, severe drought struck the state of Oklahoma, transforming once fertile farmland into dust. The storms drove farming families to California, where they became migrant workers, moving from place to place under poor conditions for very little pay.

Inspired by the plight of these workers, folk singer Woody Guthrie wrote songs about their experiences. Songs like "This Land is Your Land" and "I Ain't Got No Home" made others more aware of the troubles faced by migrant families.

What is the author's purpose for writing this passage? How do you know?

_____

_____

_____

_____

_____

What is the topic sentence of this passage?

_____

_____

_____

In your own words, tell why Woody Guthrie wrote songs about migrant workers.

_____

_____

_____

_____

_____

Reading

Many standardized tests have sections called "Reading" or "Reading Comprehension." Reading Comprehension questions test your ability to read for details, find meaning in a sentence or passage, and use context clues to figure out words or ideas you don't understand. The following is a list of topics covered on Reading Comprehension tests. Look at the tips and examples that go with each topic.

Word Meaning

Word meaning questions test your vocabulary and your ability to figure out unfamiliar words. Keep these tips in mind when answering questions about word meaning:

- Use **prefixes** and **suffixes** to help you understand a word's meaning.
- Use the surrounding words to help you guess the meaning of a new word.

Literal and Inferential Comprehension

You will be asked to read short passages and think about their meanings in two ways. In **literal comprehension** questions, you will be asked about specific details from the story. You can find the answers by going back to the passage and reading carefully. You will also be asked about the **sequence of events**—this means you will need to know the order in which events happened in the story.

In **inferential comprehension** questions, you will be required to draw conclusions or make predictions based on what you've read. These questions can be harder to answer. If you are not sure about your answers, start by eliminating unreasonable choices.

Main Idea

You will be asked to identify the main idea of some of the passages you read. The **main idea** is the message or lesson that the writer wants you to take from the passage.

Style and Genre

You will probably be asked to identify the **genre**, or category, to which a passage belongs. Genre categories include science fiction, fantasy, adventure, persuasive writing, and newspaper articles.

- You may also be asked to describe the techniques the writer uses in the passage. These may include:
  simile a comparison using *like* or *as*
  metaphor a comparison of two different objects
  personification a description that gives an object lifelike qualities
- You will probably also be asked to show whether a sentence expresses a **fact** or an **opinion**.

Reading Practice

Directions: For numbers 1 and 2, choose the word that is closest in meaning to the underlined word.

1   **a <u>stupendous</u> effort**

    Ⓐ   stupid

    Ⓑ   careless

    Ⓒ   good

    Ⓓ   terrific

2   **a serious <u>predicament</u>**

    Ⓕ   problem

    Ⓖ   predictable

    Ⓗ   party

    Ⓙ   argument

Directions: Read the passage. For numbers 3 and 4, choose the best answer to the question.

Prized Peacocks

Colorful and majestic, the peacock is one of the world's most beloved birds. Peacocks live in warm areas, such as India and Sri Lanka, where it is common to see them both in the wild and in <u>residential areas</u>. But tame peacocks can be found all over the world. This is partially because in ancient times, the bird was highly valued for its beauty. People carried the birds with them as they moved to new lands.

One thing that many people do not know is that only the male peacock spreads his back feathers in the vivid display known as his *train*. The female peacock, called a *peahen*, is generally smaller, has no train, and is less colorful. It is believed that the male peacock spreads his feathers to show off for females, but his bright coloration may also offer protection from predators when in the tropics.

3   **Which of these sentences expresses an opinion?**

    Ⓐ   The peacock is one of the world's most beloved birds.

    Ⓑ   Tame peacocks can be found all over the world.

    Ⓒ   People carried the birds with them as they moved to new lands.

    Ⓓ   The female peacock, or *peahen*, is generally smaller than the male peacock.

4   **Which best tells the meaning of <u>residential areas</u>?**

    Ⓕ   wooded areas

    Ⓖ   tropical rainforests

    Ⓗ   places where plants grow

    Ⓙ   places where people live

Language Arts

Standardized tests usually include sections that contain questions about spelling, grammar, punctuation, capitalization, and sentence structure. These sections are often called "Language Mechanics and Expression" or "Language Arts."

The following is a list of topics included under Language Mechanics and Expression. Look at the tips and examples that go with each topic. If you have trouble with one of the topics listed, talk to your teacher for extra help.

Grammar

Grammar is the set of rules that helps you write good, clear sentences. Whether you are answering a multiple choice question, writing a short answer, or responding to a writing prompt, you should:

* Remember how to use different parts of speech such as nouns, verbs, adjectives, prepositions, adverbs, and pronouns.
* Remember how to form negatives correctly.

> *correct:*   I don't know anything about the accident.
>
> *incorrect*:   I don't know nothing about the accident.

Capitalization and Punctuation

You will probably be asked specific questions about capitals and punctuation marks, but you will also be required to use them when you write answers in your own words. Keep in mind to:

Remember

* Capitalize all proper nouns and adjectives.
* Use quotation marks around the words that a character says:

> "My mother is so strict!" Callie cried.

* Use apostrophes to show possession or contraction.

> I peered into the lions' cage.
> They're always on time.

Use quotation marks around the words a character says.

Check your spelling as you write.

Language Arts

Spelling

You may be asked to pick out misspelled words or choose the correct spelling of a word that is misspelled You should also check your own spelling when you write.

incorrect Is it <u>neccesary</u> to give out the <u>adresses</u> of <u>evryone</u> on the team?

correct Is it <u>necessary</u> to give out the <u>addresses</u> of <u>everyone</u> on the team?

Sentence Structure

Remember to use complete sentences whenever you write a short answer or paragraph on a test. You may also be asked questions about individual sentences.

Keep in mind the parts of a complete sentence:

• The **subject** is the part of the sentence that is doing something.

<u>Mrs. Appleton, who lives up the street,</u> will pay me to paint her porch this summer.

• The **predicate** is the part of the sentence that tells what the subject is doing.

Mrs. Appleton, who lives up the street, <u>will pay me to paint her porch this summer.</u>

Also think about the best way to combine sentences:

• You can use connecting words such as *and*, *but*, or *although* to combine sentences.

• You can use punctuation marks such as commas or semicolons to combine sentences.

I ate all the cantaloupe. I was really hungry!

I ate all the cantaloupe <u>because</u> I was really hungry!

Remember

Use the words *and, but, because,* **and** *although,* **to combine sentences.**

Language Arts Practice

Directions: For numbers 1–4, look at the underlined part of the sentence. Choose the answer that shows the best capitalization and punctuation for that part.

1 **"larry" mary cried "aren't you forgetting something?"**

  Ⓐ "Larry, Mary cried,"
  Ⓑ "Larry," Mary cried,
  Ⓒ Larry, "Mary cried,"
  Ⓓ Correct as it is

2 **I was born in buffalo new york?**

  Ⓕ Buffalo, New York.
  Ⓖ Buffalo New York.
  Ⓗ Buffalo, new York.
  Ⓙ Correct as it is

3 **Has'nt Carol called yet?**

  Ⓐ Hasn't Carol
  Ⓑ Hasnt Carol
  Ⓒ Hasn't carol
  Ⓓ Correct as it is

4 **We had dinner at Little Sal's Pizzeria last night.**

  Ⓕ little sals pizzeria
  Ⓖ Little Sal's, pizzeria
  Ⓗ little Sals Pizzeria
  Ⓙ Correct as it is

Directions: For numbers 5–7, choose the answer that is written correctly and shows the correct capitalization and punctuation.

5 Ⓐ Have you ever seen a pink flamingo, she asked.
  Ⓑ After going to the store for groceries, I helped my brother make a delicious dinner of chicken and rice.
  Ⓒ Carmelita loves swimming; diving and boating.
  Ⓓ Because of the rainstorm, Lilly and Max, could not attend the baseball game.

6 Ⓕ Following the broadcast many people called, to complain.
  Ⓖ Chanella is a terrific flute player because: she practices every day.
  Ⓗ I couldn't believe my eyes; the judges had taped a first-prize ribbon to my project.
  Ⓙ Christopher has lived all over the country including Texas and California with his family

7 Ⓐ The new terminal is certainly long isn't it?
  Ⓑ Oh, by the way, I have to fly to Montreal in May.
  Ⓒ Our convertible has two doors but our van has four.
  Ⓓ Before you turn off the computer save your work.

Language Arts Practice

Directions: For numbers 8–11, choose the word that correctly and best completes the sentence.

8 The girls plan to open a _____ when they get older.

(F) bussiness

(G) buisness

(H) busness

(J) business

9 Nurse Louise is always _____ to the problems of her patients.

(A) simpathetic

(B) sympathitic

(C) sympathetic

(D) sympatetic

10 Thomas had no _____ from school all year.

(F) abscences

(G) abcences

(H) absenses

(J) absences

11 Before surgery, the patient received _____.

(A) anathesia

(B) anesthesia

(C) anesthisia

(D) anisthesia

Directions: For numbers 12 and 13, choose the answer that shows the best combination of the two sentences.

12 Lisa found science difficult. She got an excellent grade in the class.

(F) Lisa found science difficult because she got an excellent grade in the class.

(G) Although Lisa found science difficult, she got an excellent grade in the class.

(H) Lisa found science difficult, got an excellent grade in the class.

(J) Lisa, who found science difficult got an excellent grade in the class.

13 We can all work together to conserve water. We can all work together to conserve energy.

(A) We can all work together to conserve water and energy.

(B) We can all work together; we can all conserve water and energy.

(C) We can all work together to conserve water and work together to conserve energy.

(D) We can all work together to conserve: water and energy.

Writing

Many tests will ask you to respond to a writing prompt. A writing prompt is a question or statement that you are asked to respond to.

EXAMPLE **Think about a new way of doing something in school. Explain why your idea is a good one. Give reasons that will persuade your school to use your idea.**

The following is a list of guidelines to use when responding to a writing prompt.

Read the Prompt

- Read the instructions carefully. Sometimes you will be given a choice of questions or topics to write about. You don't want to respond to more questions than you need to.
- Once you have located the prompt to answer, read it twice to be sure you understand it. Remember, there is no one right response to a writing prompt. There are only stronger and weaker arguments.

Prewrite

- Before you write your answer, jot down some details to include.
- You may find it helpful to use a chart, web, illustration, or outline to help you organize the information you want to include in your response.
- Even if you aren't asked to, it is always a good idea to include facts and examples to support your answer. If the prompt asks you to respond to a reading passage, include specific examples from the passage to strengthen your argument.

Draft

- Begin your answer with a **topic sentence** that answers the main question and gives the main idea.
- Write **supporting sentences** that give details and tell more about your main idea. All of these sentences should relate to the topic sentence.
- If you are allowed, skip lines as you write. That way you'll have space to correct your mistakes once you're done.

Proofread

- Make sure to proofread your draft for missing words, grammar, punctuation, capitalization, indentation, and spelling. Correct your mistakes.

Writing Practice

Directions: Write a four- or five-paragraph response to *one* of the questions below.

- **Choose a television show that you would like to take off the air. Tell why you would cancel the show.**

- **Write a letter to convince your teacher that daily homework is not necessary.**

- **Describe your perfect vacation.**

_____

_____

_____

_____

_____

_____

_____

_____

_____

_____

_____

_____

_____

_____

Math: Draw a Diagram

Math Story Problems

Many standardized tests will ask you to solve math story problems. Sometimes these are also called word problems. You have probably already done problems like this in school, so this format will not be new to you. When you see story problems on a test, though, you will have limited time to find your answer.

Use the following strategies to help solve story problems quickly. Remember: not every strategy can be used with every story problem. You will have to choose the best strategy to use for each one.

Draw a Diagram

Sometimes you can draw a diagram to help solve a math problem. Diagrams are especially useful when solving geometry problems.

EXAMPLE

A rectangle has a length of 11 inches and a width of 1 foot, 3 inches. What is the area of the rectangle?

Ⓐ 33 square inches
Ⓑ 165 inches
Ⓒ 165 square inches
Ⓓ 33 square feet

• Draw a diagram of the rectangle and label it with information from the problem.

• Recall the formula for finding area: *length × width = area*. Fill in this formula with information from the problem, making sure that all your numbers are expressed in the same units:

11 inches × 1 foot, 3 inches = area
Since 1 foot, 3 inches equals 15 inches, I will rewrite the formula
using 15 inches: 11 × 15 = 165

• As you examine the answer choices, pay close attention to the unit label after each. Many tests try to trick you by giving incorrectly labeled choices. Since area is expressed in square inches, centimeters, and so on, you can eliminate any choices that do not have "square" in the label. So while there are two choices that contain 165, you know that **C** must be the answer.

When you draw a diagram:

☐ Read the problem carefully.
☐ Determine what data you need to solve the problem.
☐ Draw a diagram based on the data.
☐ Use the data in your diagram to solve the problem.
☐ Choose the answer with the correct unit.

Diagram Practice

Directions: For numbers 1–4, choose the best answer to each question. Draw a diagram to help you solve each problem.

1 Carrie has a box with a length of 5 inches, a width of 12 inches, and height of 4 inches. What is the volume of the box?

 Ⓐ 21 square inches

 Ⓑ 42 cubic inches

 Ⓒ 240 square inches

 Ⓓ 240 cubic inches

2 Olde Town Restaurant sells a vegetable pizza that is 18 inches in diameter. What is the area of the pizza?

 Ⓕ   254.34 square inches

 Ⓖ   798.63 square inches

 Ⓗ   798.63 cubic inches

 Ⓙ 1017.36 cubic inches

3 Billy just bought a new aquarium for his goldfish, Baxter. The aquarium is 10 inches high, 8 inches wide, and 2 feet long. If Billy wants to fill the tank half full of water, how much will he need?

 Ⓐ 1920 cubic inches

 Ⓑ   960 cubic inches

 Ⓒ   82 cubic inches

 Ⓓ   41 square inches

4 Four boys held a race. Ramik ran the race in 1 minute and 18 seconds. Louie, who came in last, finished 6 seconds after Ramik. Tito finished the race 18 seconds ahead of Louie. Scott finished the race 9 seconds ahead of Ramik. Who won?

 Ⓕ Louie

 Ⓖ Scott

 Ⓗ Ramik

 Ⓙ Tito

Math: Trick Questions

Some test questions contain the word *not*. You must be careful to notice when the word *not* is used. These are a type of trick question; you are being tested to see if you have read and understood the material completely.

EXAMPLE **Which number is *not* equivalent to 16.15?**

    Ⓐ $16\frac{3}{20}$

    Ⓑ $\frac{323}{20}$

    Ⓒ $\frac{1615}{100}$

    Ⓓ $\frac{1.615}{10}$

- When solving this type of problem, first figure out how the word *not* applies to the problem. In this case you must find the number that is not equivalent to 16.15.
- Check the possible answers to see which one is not equivalent to 16.15:
- $16\frac{3}{20}$ is the mixed-number equivalent to 16.15.
- $\frac{323}{20}$ is an improper fraction for 16.15.
- $\frac{1615}{100}$ is a fraction for 16.15 that isn't expressed in lowest terms.
- $\frac{1.615}{10}$ is not equivalent to 16.15.
- The correct answer is **D**, since the other choices are all equivalent to 16.15.

Remember

Watch out for trick questions, especially those that have the word *not* in them.

When you have the word *not* in a problem:

☐ Read the problem carefully.
☐ Determine what information you need to solve the problem.
☐ Compare all of the possible answer choices.
☐ Solve the problem.

Trick Questions Practice

Directions: Look for the word *not* as you answer numbers 1–6.

1 Which solid shape does not have more than four faces?

Ⓐ a rectangular prism
Ⓑ a cube
Ⓒ a pyramid
Ⓓ a cylinder

2 Which of these angles is not obtuse?

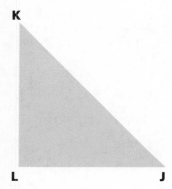

Ⓕ angle J
Ⓖ angle K
Ⓗ angle L
Ⓙ all of the above

3 Marcus earned $15 per weekday at his summer job and $15 plus 50% on weekend days. If he worked for 18 weekdays and 5 weekend days, how much did he earn?

Ⓐ $345.00
Ⓑ $347.50
Ⓒ $382.50
Ⓓ $517.50

4 The town of Bronson has 25,232 residents. 6,470 residents voted to build a new town hall. 3,911 residents voted against building a new town hall. 852 people voted to postpone the decision for another year. How many residents of Bronson did not vote?

Ⓕ 10,831
Ⓖ 11,233
Ⓗ 13,999
Ⓙ 18,762

5 Which of the following number sentences is not true?

Ⓐ $\frac{3}{8} < \frac{3}{4}$
Ⓑ $\frac{1}{3} < \frac{2}{5}$
Ⓒ $\frac{5}{9} < \frac{1}{6}$
Ⓓ $\frac{10}{7} < \frac{19}{10}$

6 An office has 52 workers. There are three times as many men as women. How many workers are not women?

Ⓕ 13
Ⓖ 39
Ⓗ 17
Ⓙ 15

Math: Paper and Pencil

On tests it often helps to work a problem out using paper and pencil. This helps you to visualize the problem and double-check your answer. It is especially useful when you must solve an equation.

> **EXAMPLE** Marie's cat, Clyde, ate $\frac{1}{2}$ cup of cat food each day for the entire month of June. In July, Clyde ate $\frac{3}{4}$ cup of cat food each day. How much cat food did Clyde eat altogether in June and July?
>
> _____

- Here you are not given any answers to choose from; you must figure out the answer using a paper and pencil.
- First you must remember that there are 30 days in June and 31 days in July. Write and solve equations to figure out how much cat food was eaten in each month:

> 30 days × $\frac{1}{2}$ cup of cat food per day = $\frac{30}{2}$ cups or 15 cups
>
> 31 days × $\frac{3}{4}$ cup of cat food per day = $\frac{93}{4}$ cups or 23$\frac{1}{4}$ cups

- Then add the total number of cups together:

> 15 + 23$\frac{1}{4}$ = 38$\frac{1}{4}$ cups

- Now use paper and pencil again to check the answer you found the first time.
- You know the answer is 38$\frac{1}{4}$ cups of cat food.

When you use pencil and paper:
- ☐ Read the problem carefully.
- ☐ Write neatly so that you do not make errors.
- ☐ Solve the problem.
- ☐ Check your work.

Paper and Pencil Practice

Directions: Use the work area to show your work as you solve numbers 1–6.

1 It takes Saturn 29.5 years to orbit the sun. How many times does Saturn orbit the sun in 375 years?

_____

1

2 Phillipe bought a new pair of sneakers for $49. The following week, the same sneakers went on sale for 25% off. How much money could Phillipe have saved if he had waited until the shoes went on sale?

_____

2

3 What is the volume of this shape? _____

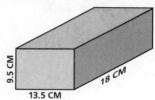

3

4 352.56 ×92.7 = _____

4

5 Michele received the following scores on science tests this year: 89%, 78%, 92%, 81%, 95%. What was Michele's average in science?

_____

5

6 Last year, Theo had a free throw average of 65%. If he took 160 free throws all year, how many shots did he make?

_____

6

Math: Guess and Check

One way to solve a word problem is to make your best guess and then work backwards to check your answer. This is a good strategy to use when you are not exactly sure how to solve a problem.

EXAMPLE **11 less than 2.5 times x is 9. What is x?**

Ⓐ 20

Ⓑ 10

Ⓒ 8

Ⓓ 2

- First, try choosing the best answer from the choices you have been given. Imagine that your guess for this answer is **B**, 10.

 **Remember**

$$2.5 \times 10 = 25$$
$$25 - 11 = 14$$

- Since your answer was too big, you know you should try a smaller number. Guess **C**, 8. Plug it into your equation.

Sometimes it's OK to guess. Then work backwards to make sure your guess is reasonable.

$$2.5 \times 8 = 20$$
$$20 - 11 = 9$$

- So 8 works in this problem; as working backwards showed, the correct answer is **C**.

 When you use the guess and check method:
- ☐ Read the problem carefully.
- ☐ Make a reasonable first guess.
- ☐ Revise your guess based on whether your answer was too high or low.
- ☐ Check that your answer is reasonable based on the question.

Guess and Check Practice

Directions: For numbers 1–6, use the guess-and-check method to figure out your answers.

1 Pamela made 5 cheese sandwiches, 6 peanut butter sandwiches, and 1 tuna sandwich to bring on a picnic with her friends. If there is enough for each person to have exactly one and a half sandwiches, how many people will there be on the picnic?

　Ⓐ　7
　Ⓑ　8
　Ⓒ　12
　Ⓓ　18

2 Triangle XYZ has two equal angles. Angles X and Z both measure 60 degrees less than angle Y. What is the measure of angle X?

　Ⓕ　30
　Ⓖ　40
　Ⓗ　60
　Ⓙ　80

3 Triangle Q has two angles of 30 degrees each. What is the measure of the third angle?

　Ⓐ　60 degrees
　Ⓑ　120 degrees
　Ⓒ　150 degrees
　Ⓓ　300 degrees

4 Two numbers have a product of 104,976 and a quotient of 16. What are the two numbers?

　Ⓕ　16 and 81
　Ⓖ　1296 and 16
　Ⓗ　1296 and 81
　Ⓙ　104,976 and 9

5 A cube has a volume of 2,197 cubic feet. How long is one side of the cube?

　Ⓐ　5 feet
　Ⓑ　13 feet
　Ⓒ　20 feet
　Ⓓ　27 feet

6 Bruno's Bakery sells 1,500 dinner rolls per day. 62% of the rolls are sold to restaurants. 17% are sold to hospitals. The rest are sold to individual customers who walk into the bakery. How many rolls are sold to walk-in customers?

　Ⓕ　255 rolls
　Ⓖ　315 rolls
　Ⓗ　930 rolls
　Ⓙ　1185 rolls

Math: Estimation

Use estimation to help you narrow down answer choices on a multiple choice test. Some tests also ask you to choose the best estimate for a test question instead of finding the correct answer.

> **EXAMPLE** **Jill wants to buy a new bike lock. The lock costs $19.59. If Jill earns $3.75 per day, how long will it take her to save up enough money for the new lock?**
>
> Ⓐ 4 days
> Ⓑ 6 days
> Ⓒ 10 days
> Ⓓ 2 weeks

- First, estimate the answer by rounding up or down. Round to the most precise place needed for the problem. In this case, to the nearest dollar.

    $19.59 rounds up to $20
    $ 3.75 rounds up to $4
    At $4 per day, it would take about 5 days to save $20.

- You can cross off choices **C** and **D** since they are far out of your estimated range.
- Now you must choose between **A** and **B**, as both are close to your estimate. Do the math to find out if the first choice could work in the problem:

    $3.75 ×4 = 15

- The equation shows that 4 does not work because the amount of money saved in four days is lower than the cost of the lock. So the answer must be **B**, 6 days.

When you estimate and answer:
- ☐ Read the problem carefully.
- ☐ Round the numbers you need to estimate the answer.
- ☐ Estimate the answer.
- ☐ Eliminate any answers not close to your estimate.
- ☐ If necessary, find the exact answer.

Estimation Practice

Directions: For numbers 1–3, choose the best estimate for each question.

Directions: For numbers 4–6, use estimation to figure out the correct answer.

1 Veronica is head of the girls' softball team. Last season she took 522 pitches and hit 137 fair balls. What was her approximate batting average?

Ⓐ .260

Ⓑ .360

Ⓒ .367

Ⓓ .407

2 A total of 31,012 people flew on Big Sky airlines last year. Of that number, 6% flew first class and 11% flew business class. The rest flew coach class. Approximately how many people flew coach class?

Ⓕ 25,740 people

Ⓖ 26,350 people

Ⓗ 29,250 people

Ⓙ 30,200 people

3 Suppose you deposit $700 in a savings account at $5\frac{1}{2}\%$ interest. About how much interest will you receive in one year?

Ⓐ $35.00

Ⓑ $36.50

Ⓒ $38.50

Ⓓ $39.00

4 How many hours are there in 61 days?

Ⓕ 1440 hours

Ⓖ 1464 hours

Ⓗ 1848 hours

Ⓙ   48 hours

5 A circle has a radius of 5 centimeters. What is the area of the circle?

Ⓐ   15.7 square centimeters

Ⓑ   75.0 square centimeters

Ⓒ   78.5 square centimeters

Ⓓ 100.0 square centimeters

6 Tamara makes a CD with 4 songs on it. The first song is 8 minutes and 32 seconds long; the next is 6 minutes and 14 seconds long; the third is 4 minutes and 47 seconds long; the last is 9 minutes and 51 seconds long. What is the average length of a song on Tamara's CD?

Ⓕ 6 minutes, 22 seconds

Ⓖ 7 minutes, 21 seconds

Ⓗ 7 minutes, 40 seconds

Ⓙ 8 minutes, 5 seconds

Math: Incomplete Information

Some test problems may include "not enough information" as one of the answer choices. When you see a problem with this as an answer choice, watch out! The problem may not contain enough information for you to solve it.

EXAMPLE **What is the area of this triangle?**

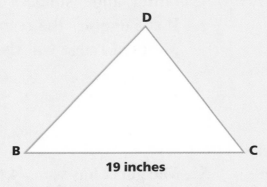

19 inches

Ⓐ 78 square inches
Ⓑ 63 square inches
Ⓒ 47 square inches
Ⓓ Not enough information

- Determine what information is given in the problem and the picture: A triangle is shown. To find the area, you must multiply one half of the base times the height of the triangle. The base of the triangle is 19 inches long, but the height is not given.
- Since the height of the triangle is not given, you should try to see if there is another way to figure it out. However, there is no other information; you cannot solve the problem. So **D** is your answer.

When you think you don't have enough information to solve a problem:
- ☐ Read the problem carefully.
- ☐ Determine what information you need to solve the problem.
- ☐ Check to see if you have all the information to solve the problem.
- ☐ Verify that the information you need to solve the problem is missing.

Incomplete Information Practice

Directions: For numbers 1–6, decide whether each problem gives enough information. Choose the correct answer.

1 There are 27 students in Mr. Dunbar's science class. If $\frac{1}{3}$ of the class goes on a field trip, how many will be left over?

- Ⓐ 9 students
- Ⓑ 12 students
- Ⓒ 18 students
- Ⓓ Not enough information

2 Allen lives 15 blocks from Michael's house. Michael lives 6 blocks from Tina's house. How far away from Tina's house does Allen live?

- Ⓕ 9 blocks
- Ⓖ 15 blocks
- Ⓗ 21 blocks
- Ⓙ Not enough information

3 In September, a potato chip factory produced 2 tons of barbecue potato chips, 1 ton of sour cream and onion chips, and 5 tons of plain chips. The same factory produced 2 tons of barbecue chips, 2 tons of sour cream and onion chips, and 8 tons of plain chips in October. What percentage of the total chips produced by the factory that year was barbecue flavored?

- Ⓐ 10%
- Ⓑ 15%
- Ⓒ 20%
- Ⓓ Not enough information

4 Carla's fudge recipe calls for 2 cups sugar, $\frac{2}{3}$ cup cream, 1 tablespoon butter, and 2 squares of chocolate. If she doubles the recipe, how many pieces of fudge will she have?

- Ⓕ 16 pieces
- Ⓖ 32 pieces
- Ⓗ 64 pieces
- Ⓙ Not enough information

5 Margaret has won 24 tennis tournaments, more than any other female tennis player in her school. Steffi has won the second highest number of tournaments. How many has she won?

- Ⓐ 22 tournaments
- Ⓑ 20 tournaments
- Ⓒ 15 tournaments
- Ⓓ Not enough information

6 It takes about eight minutes for a ray of light to travel from the sun to the Earth. If Pluto is 40 times farther away from the sun than Earth is, about how long does it take for a ray of light to travel from the sun to Pluto?

- Ⓕ about 32 minutes
- Ⓖ about 2 hours, 10 minutes
- Ⓗ about 5 hours, 20 minutes
- Ⓙ Not enough information

Math: Using a Calculator

You may be allowed to use a calculator with some standardized tests. Using a calculator can save you time, especially when you need to compute multi-digit numbers. A calculator can also allow you to double-check your work quickly.

> **EXAMPLE** $31^4 =$
>
> - (A)   15
> - (B)   124
> - (C)   923,521
> - (D)   28,629,151

Exponent: the number that tells how many times to use the base number as the factor

- To solve the problem, you must write the multiplication sentence in which 31 is shown four times:

$$31 \times 31 \times 31 \times 31 = \text{?}$$

The correct answer is **C**.

- Be sure to key in the correct numbers to find the correct answer!

When you use a calculator:
- ☐ Read the problem carefully.
- ☐ Be sure you key in the correct numbers.
- ☐ Solve the problem.
- ☐ Check to see that your answer is reasonable.

Calculator Practice

Directions: For numbers 1–7, choose the correct answer.

1 $52\sqrt{81} =$

- Ⓐ   1.6
- Ⓑ   133.0
- Ⓒ   468.0
- Ⓓ   4212.0

2 **36% of 795 =**

- Ⓕ   286.2
- Ⓖ   202.2
- Ⓗ   28.6
- Ⓙ   22.1

3 The area of a building is 27^3 feet. What is the area of the building?

- Ⓐ   27 square feet
- Ⓑ   108 square feet
- Ⓒ   729 square feet
- Ⓓ   19,683 square feet

4 $\dfrac{(2.51 - 1.11)}{(8.15 + 3.15)} =$

- Ⓕ   .12
- Ⓖ   8.07
- Ⓗ   9.90
- Ⓙ   15.82

5 The length of one side of a cube equals 23.7 centimeters. What is the volume of the cube?

- Ⓐ   71.1 cubic centimeters
- Ⓑ   561.7 cubic centimeters
- Ⓒ   13,312.1 cubic centimeters
- Ⓓ   16,384.7 cubic centimeters

6 Vanessa has $72.55 in her savings account. Horatio has more than three times as much in his savings account as Vanessa has. Ronald has exactly half the amount that Horatio has. What is the least amount of money that the three friends could have altogether?

- Ⓕ $292.24
- Ⓖ $290.02
- Ⓗ $326.49
- Ⓙ $399.04

7 $16^5 =$

- Ⓐ   4,096
- Ⓑ   65,536
- Ⓒ   1,048,576
- Ⓓ   80

Math: Computation

Most standardized tests contain math sections where you must solve number equations. These questions test your ability to find exact answers to math problems. You will often be allowed to use scrap paper to work out these problems, but the work you show on scrap paper will not count.

Using Operations

Your ability to perform basic mathematical operations (such as addition, subtraction, multiplication, and division) will be tested. Whenever you are solving a math equation, be sure of which operation you must use to solve the problem. These are skills you may be tested on:

- adding and subtracting with whole numbers, decimals, fractions, and negative numbers
- multiplying and dividing with fractions
- multiplying and dividing with decimals to the thousandths place
- calculating to powers of ten

Even though you will be given answer choices, it's best to work out the problem first using scrap paper. Then you can compare the answer you found to the choices that are given.

Other Things to Keep in Mind

If your problem contains units, be sure that you find the answer choice with the correct units labeled. Many tests will try to confuse you by substituting one unit for another in an answer choice.

Finally, if you get to a tough problem, look carefully at the answer choices and use logic to decide which one makes the most sense. Then plug this choice into the equation and see if it works.

Remember

It's always a good idea to work out the problem first using scrap paper.

Computation Practice

Directions: For numbers 1–10, choose the correct answer.

1 $3.372 \div 0.6 =$

  Ⓐ 5.620
  Ⓑ 0.562
  Ⓒ 0.056
  Ⓓ 0.006

2 $36 + {}^-45 =$

  Ⓕ 9
  Ⓖ ${}^-9$
  Ⓗ 81
  Ⓙ ${}^-81$

3 $7(5-8) =$

  Ⓐ 21
  Ⓑ ${}^-21$
  Ⓒ 91
  Ⓓ ${}^-91$

4 $3\frac{5}{6} + 5\frac{1}{4} =$

  Ⓕ $8\frac{5}{6}$
  Ⓖ 9
  Ⓗ $9\frac{1}{12}$
  Ⓙ $9\frac{1}{6}$

5 $392 \times 67 =$

  Ⓐ 2626.4
  Ⓑ 26,264
  Ⓒ 26,164
  Ⓓ 5.85

6 $25^3 =$

  Ⓕ 625
  Ⓖ 15,625
  Ⓗ 15,675
  Ⓙ None of the above

7 $1.72 \times .34 =$

  Ⓐ 584.8
  Ⓑ 58.48
  Ⓒ 5.848
  Ⓓ 0.5848

8 $\frac{3}{8} \div \frac{4}{5} =$

  Ⓕ $\frac{15}{32}$
  Ⓖ $\frac{3}{10}$
  Ⓗ $\frac{17}{40}$
  Ⓙ $1\frac{5}{8}$

9 $\frac{3}{4} \times \frac{1}{2} \times \frac{3}{5} =$

  Ⓐ $\frac{7}{11}$
  Ⓑ $1\frac{17}{20}$
  Ⓒ $\frac{9}{40}$
  Ⓓ None of the above

10 $5\frac{1}{2} \times 3\frac{1}{6} =$

  Ⓕ $8\frac{2}{3}$
  Ⓖ $17\frac{5}{12}$
  Ⓗ $15\frac{1}{12}$
  Ⓙ $15\frac{2}{3}$

Math: Concepts

Standardized tests also check your understanding of important math concepts you will have learned about in school.

Number Concepts

You may have to show that you understand the following number concepts:

- using negative numbers
- finding percents and decimal/percent equivalents
- finding common factors
- calculating averages
- naming the factors of a number
- ordering integers
- finding square roots
- standard and metric measure equivalents

Geometry

It's also common to see questions about geometry on standardized tests. You may be asked to:

- recognize parallel and perpendicular lines, rays, and segments.
- find the area and perimeter of flat shapes.
- find the volume of a solid shape.
- find the line of symmetry in a flat shape.
- recognize right, obtuse, and acute angles.
- understand congruence.

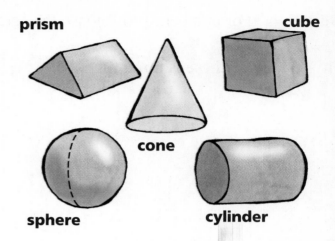

prism cube cone sphere cylinder

Other Things to Keep in Mind

The best way to prepare for concept questions is to study math words and definitions in advance. However, if you come to a difficult problem, think of what you do know about the topic and eliminate answer choices that don't make sense. For example, if you are asked to identify a shape that you don't recognize, you may recognize some of other shapes mentioned and know that they couldn't be correct. Use the process of elimination whenever you come to a tough question.

Remember

Study math words and definition in advance.

Eliminate answer choices that don't make sense.

Concepts Practice

Directions: For numbers 1–6, choose the correct answer to each problem.

1 **Which of these is not a factor of 2478?**

Ⓐ 7
Ⓑ 42
Ⓒ 32
Ⓓ 59

2 **Which of the following lines are parallel?**

Ⓕ

Ⓗ

Ⓖ

Ⓙ

3 **The square root of 144 =**

Ⓐ   8
Ⓑ   12
Ⓒ 20,736
Ⓓ None of the above

4 **74% is another way to write**

Ⓕ 7.4
Ⓖ .074
Ⓗ .74
Ⓙ $\frac{74}{1000}$

5 **Which of the following does *not* equal 1250 centimeters?**

Ⓐ 12.5 meters
Ⓑ 12500 millimeters
Ⓒ 125 decimeters
Ⓓ 1.25 kilometers

6 **Which of the following is an acute angle?**

Ⓕ

Ⓖ

Ⓗ

Ⓙ

Math: Applications

You will often be asked to apply what you know about math to a new type of problem or set of information. Even if you aren't exactly sure how to solve a problem of this type, you can usually draw on what you already know to make the most logical choice.

When preparing for standardized tests, you may want to practice some of the following:

- solving equations with multiple steps and/or operations
- recognizing number patterns
- using the correct order of operations
- using a number line with whole numbers and decimals
- reading bar graphs, tally charts, or pictographs
- reading pie charts
- reading line and double-line graphs
- reading and making Venn diagrams
- plotting x-y coordinates
- finding ratios
- finding probability

Other Things to Keep in Mind

When answering application questions, be sure to read each problem carefully. You may want to use scrap paper to work out some problems.

Again, if you come to a problem you aren't sure how to solve or a word/idea you don't recognize, try to eliminate answer choices by using what you do know. Then go back and check your answer choice in the context of the problem.

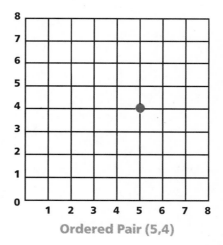

Ordered Pair (5,4)

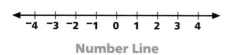

Number Line

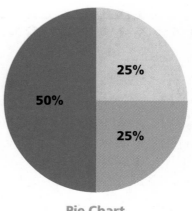

Pie Chart

Applications Practice

Directions: For numbers 1–5, choose the correct answer.

1 **What is the next number in this pattern?**

3, 6, 12, 24, 48, _____

Ⓐ 80
Ⓑ 88
Ⓒ 96
Ⓓ None of the above

2 **What are the coordinates of point M?**

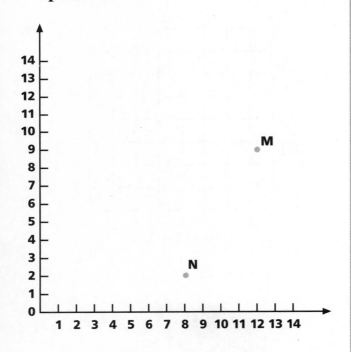

Ⓕ (8, 2)
Ⓖ (2, 8)
Ⓗ (12, 9)
Ⓙ (9, 12)

3 **There are 17 boys and 12 girls in Ms. Hamilton's gym class. Three boys are out sick on Tuesday, and Ms. Hamilton is picking teams at random for a game of volleyball. What is the probability that she will pick a girl first?**

Ⓐ $\frac{12}{17}$ Ⓒ $\frac{12}{14}$
Ⓑ $\frac{6}{13}$ Ⓓ $\frac{6}{7}$

4 **If you wanted to show how the population of a city changed over time, which would be the best type of graphic to use?**

Ⓕ a Venn diagram
Ⓖ a pictograph
Ⓗ a pie chart
Ⓙ a line graph

5 **Point X is before point D but after point B. Which of these could not contain point X?**

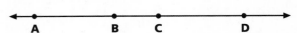

Ⓐ $\overline{AD}$

Ⓑ $\overline{BD}$

Ⓒ $\overline{BC}$

Ⓓ $\overline{AB}$

Social Studies

Standardized tests often include questions about social studies topics. You may see questions about maps, geography, history, and government.

The following is a list of topics that may be covered on the test and tips to use when solving the questions. Sample questions are also included.

Map Skills

You will probably be asked to look at a map and answer questions about it. Keep these tips in mind:

- All maps include a **compass rose**, a **legend** with **symbols**, and a **scale**.
- **Lines of latitude** (horizontal) and **longitude** (vertical) are the grid lines on maps that help to describe the location of specific places.
- Different maps serve different purposes, such as **political maps**, **physical maps**, **relief maps**, **population maps,** and **topographical maps**.

When you read a map, be sure to read the title first so that you understand the kind of information that is being presented.

Geography

Geography is the study of the land and its features. You should know these terms:

- **natural features:** plateau, peninsula, isthmus, butte, cape, delta, dune, strait, mesa, archipelago, savanna, tributary
- **other geography terms:** hemisphere, equator, prime meridian, latitude, longitude

You may be required to answer questions about U.S. geography, such as the locations, features, and capitals of different states. You should also be able to locate each of the seven continents on a map, as well as important countries and cities of the world.

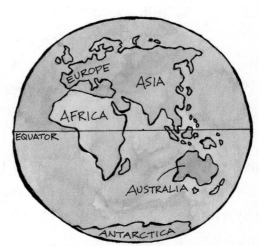

EASTERN HEMISPHERE

Compass Rose

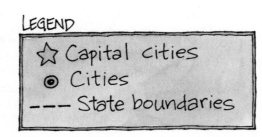

Social Studies

Time Lines

A **time line** organizes historical events in chronological order. Some questions will ask you to use a time line to answer a question.

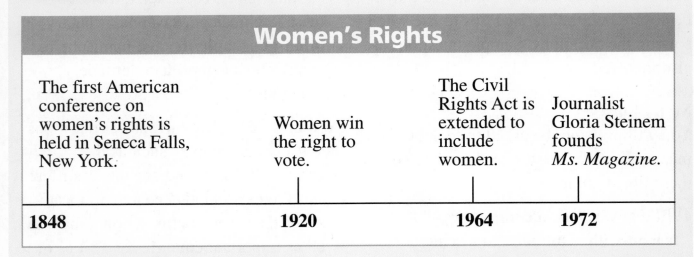

Women's Rights

The first American conference on women's rights is held in Seneca Falls, New York.	Women win the right to vote.	The Civil Rights Act is extended to include women.	Journalist Gloria Steinem founds *Ms. Magazine.*
1848	**1920**	**1964**	**1972**

Which event took place only after women won the right to vote?

Ⓐ The first conference on women's rights is held.

Ⓑ An amendment is written to protect women's rights in the workplace.

Ⓒ The first woman vice-president was elected.

Ⓓ None of the above

You can eliminate **A** because this event took place before women won the right to vote; you can eliminate **C** because this event has not ever happened. But the time line shows that an amendment was added to the Constitution to protect women's rights in 1964. So the correct answer is **B**.

When you see a time line on a test:
☐ Pay careful attention to the dates given in the time line.
☐ Note the order of events that are given.

Social Studies

Reading Passages

You will probably be asked to read a passage about a social studies topic and to answer questions about it. Keep these tips in mind:

- Before you read, look at the questions first so that you know what kind of information you are looking for.
- Look for key words: *who, what, when, where,* and *why.* These will help you focus on the relevant information in the passage.
- As you read, keep in mind the purpose of the passage. Ask yourself: what does the writer want me to learn?

Research Skills

Some questions will test your ability to think like a historian. You will be asked about different sources that historians use to find out historical data. You may need to know:

- different factual sources for doing historical research, like books, encyclopedias, and newspaper articles
- parts of books that help you do research effectively, like a table of contents or an index

Social Studies Knowledge

Some social studies questions will ask specific questions about topics you have been studying in class, such as:

- the Constitution and the Declaration of Independence
- the American Revolution
- events in the early history of the nation including the War of 1812, development of transportation infrastructure, and immigration
- events of the mid-nineteenth century including Westward expansion, regional disputes between North and South, the abolition movement, and causes of the Civil War
- Reconstruction
- causes and effects of the Industrial Revolution

As you answer these questions, make sure you understand what the question is asking. Get rid of the unreasonable answers first, and then make your best guess.

Remember

Before you read a passage, look at the questions first so that you will know what kind of information you are looking for.

Social Studies Practice

Directions: For numbers 1–3, choose the best answer to each question.

1 **The General who lead American forces to victory in the Revolutionary War was**

Ⓐ Paul Revere.

Ⓑ George Washington.

Ⓒ King George III.

Ⓓ Charles Cornwallis.

2 **The United States went to war with Britain in 1812 to**

Ⓕ protest Britain's maritime policies.

Ⓖ acquire the Mississippi Territory.

Ⓗ gain independence for the colonies.

Ⓙ establish the right to trade with other British colonies.

3 **The abolition movement fought to**

Ⓐ win the right to vote for women.

Ⓑ prohibit the sale of alcohol in the United States.

Ⓒ end slavery.

Ⓓ set aside land for displaced Native Americans.

Directions: Study the time line. For questions 4 and 5, choose the best answer to each question.

Civil War				
The Civil War officially begins.	The Emancipation Proclamation is issued.	Abraham Lincoln is re-elected.	Abraham Lincoln is assassinated.	The Civil War ends.
April 1861	**January 1863**	**November 1864**	**April 1865**	**May 1865**

4 **How long after the start of the Civil War did Lincoln issue the Emancipation Proclamation?**

Ⓕ four months   Ⓖ nine months   Ⓗ twenty-one months   Ⓙ two years

5 **Which of the following happened only after Lincoln was assassinated?**

Ⓐ the Civil War began

Ⓑ the Civil War ended

Ⓒ the Emancipation Proclamation was issued

Ⓓ Lincoln was re-elected

Social Studies Practice

Directions: Read the passage. Then choose the best answer for numbers 1 and 2.

Molasses Flood

Today, sugar is America's most popular sweetener. But one hundred years ago, Americans favored molasses, a sticky brown liquid with a consistency like thick maple syrup. At that time, Boston, Massachusetts, was one of the nation's leading producers of molasses. Its shores were lined with molasses factories and warehouses.

On one January day in 1919, a tragedy struck the city of Boston. A 58-foot tall tank of molasses exploded, sending over two million gallons of hot liquid out onto city streets. The explosion created a wave of molasses over 10 feet tall, moving at a breakneck speed of 35 miles per hour. People and horses were trapped in the boiling goo, and buildings were brought crashing to the ground. The wave of molasses even flooded the Public Works department, killing workmen as they ate their lunches inside. By the time the melee was over, 21 people had been killed and over 150 people injured. It took more than 6 months to clean up the giant, sticky mess.

There have been several theories about what caused the tank to explode. One possibility is that the tank was overfilled with molasses to prepare for a possible shortage. Another theory claimed that someone used a dynamite bomb to explode it. Some people even felt that a rapid rise in the temperature outside caused the molasses to expand, putting pressure on the tank. But the most likely explanation is also the simplest one; the tank just wasn't strong enough.

1 **Which of the following was not a result of the molasses tank explosion?**

Ⓐ 21 people were killed.

Ⓑ The Public Works building was flooded.

Ⓒ There was a possible shortage of molasses.

Ⓓ There have been several theories about the cause of the explosion.

2 **In which of the following reference sources would you be most likely to find this passage?**

Ⓕ an encyclopedia

Ⓖ an atlas

Ⓗ a dictionary

Ⓙ an almanac

Science

You will often see science questions on standardized tests. These questions may be about scientific facts. They may also test your ability to "think like a scientist." This means you must use data (information) to make predictions and draw conclusions.

Science Vocabulary

Many science questions will include at least one of the words below:

research question: the question that a scientist asks

hypothesis: a scientist's possible answer to the question

experiment: a test to see if the hypothesis is correct

prediction: a guess about the future results of an experiment

observation: when a scientist watches the results of an experiment

data: the information collected in an experiment

conclusion: a statement based on information gathered in an experiment

Science Knowledge

Science questions on your standardized test may require you to know specific scientific information. This may include information about:

- forces and motion (velocity, gravity)
- cell biology (plant cells vs. animal cells, cell parts)
- the physical and chemical properties of substances
- composition of atoms including protons, neutrons, and electrons; the composition of compounds; the law of conservation of matter
- role of carbon in the chemistry of living organisms
- structure and function of the periodic table
- different features of the universe such as galaxies, comets, asteroids, and planetary satellites

If you don't know the answer to a specific question, use your common sense. An excellent strategy is to eliminate unreasonable answers first.

Science

Reading Graphs

Standardized tests will often include graphs showing the results of an experiment. You may be asked to read the graph or to use the data to predict or draw a conclusion. Look at this example:

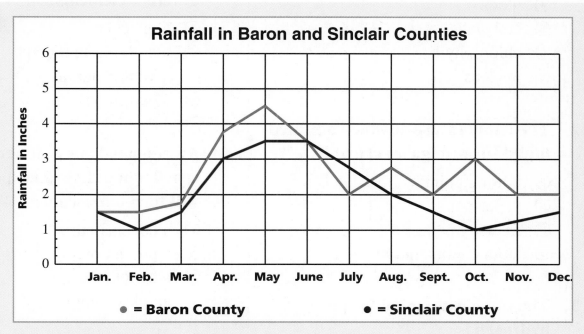

Which month shows the greatest difference in rainfall between Baron and Sinclair counties?

Ⓐ March   Ⓒ May

Ⓑ October   Ⓓ Not enough information

You can see that there are two sets of data on this line graph, one showing rainfall for Baron County and the other showing rainfall for Sinclair County. The question asks you to find the month with the greatest difference in rainfall, so you will be looking for the place on the graph in which the lines are furthest apart. You can see that spot near the end of the graph, over the notch for the month of October. So the correct answer is **B**, October.

Science Processes

Some science questions will ask you to answer questions about the scientific process. Keep in mind the steps of a scientific experiment and use your common sense as you examine your choices.

Science Practice

Directions: For numbers 1–7, choose the best answer to each question.

1 The central part of a plant or animal cell is called the

Ⓐ atom.
Ⓑ cell wall.
Ⓒ chlorophyll.
Ⓓ nucleus.

2 The temperature at which a heated liquid turns to gas is called its

Ⓕ boiling point.
Ⓖ vapor point.
Ⓗ freezing point.
Ⓙ atomic temperature.

3 The chemical symbol for pure hydrogen is

Ⓐ H_2O
Ⓑ Hg
Ⓒ H
Ⓓ H_2

4 Which of the following does not normally orbit the sun?

Ⓕ a comet
Ⓖ the moon
Ⓗ Pluto
Ⓙ Earth

5 What type of graph would be best to compare the atomic weights of different elements?

Ⓐ a pie chart
Ⓑ a multiple-line graph
Ⓒ a Venn diagram
Ⓓ a bar graph

6 An educated guess, that can be tested, about how an experiment will turn out is called

Ⓕ a conclusion.
Ⓖ a prediction.
Ⓗ a hypothesis.
Ⓙ an observation.

7 Which of the following is not a type of rock?

Ⓐ igneous
Ⓑ sedimentary
Ⓒ metamorphic
Ⓓ crystal

Practice Test and Final Test Information

The remainder of this book is made up of two tests. On page 79, you will find a Practice Test. On page 125, you will find a Final Test. These tests will give you a chance to put the tips you have learned to work. There is also a name and answer sheet preceding each test and an answer key at the end of the book.

Here are some things to remember as you take these tests:

• Be sure you understand all the directions before you begin each test.

• Ask an adult questions about the directions if you do not understand them.

• Work as quickly as you can during each test. There are no time limits on the Practice Test, but you should try to make good use of your time. There are suggested time limits on the Final Test to give you practice managing your time.

• You will notice little GO and STOP signs at the bottom of the test pages. When you see a GO sign, continue on to the next page if you feel ready. The STOP sign means you are at the end of a section. When you see a STOP sign, take a break.

• When you change an answer, be sure to erase your first mark completely.

• You can guess at an answer or skip difficult items and go back to them later.

• Use the tips you have learned whenever you can.

• After you have completed your tests, check your answers with the answer key. You can record the number of questions you got correct for each unit on the recording sheet on page 76.

• It is OK to be a little nervous. You may even do better.

• When you complete all the lessons in this book, you will be on your way to test success!

Table of Contents

Name Sheet

This is a practice name sheet like the ones you will use in school. Follow these directions:

1. Use a No. 2 pencil.
2. Write your name in the boxes. Put only **one letter** in each box. Then fill in one little circle below each letter that matches that letter of your name.
3. Fill in all the other information.

	STUDENT'S NAME				SCHOOL		

A letter grid for LAST name, FIRST name, and MI with bubbles A through Z.

SCHOOL

TEACHER

FEMALE ○   MALE ○

BIRTHDATE

MONTH	DAY	YEAR
JAN ○	0 0	0
FEB ○	1 1	1
MAR ○	2 2	2
APR ○	3 3	3
MAY ○	4	4
JUN ○	5	5 5
JUL ○	6	6 6
AUG ○	7	7 7
SEP ○	8	8 8
OCT ○	9	9 9
NOV ○		
DEC ○		

GRADE

④   ⑤   ⑥   ⑦   ⑧

Record Your Scores

After you have completed and checked each test, record your scores below. Do not count your answers for the sample questions or the writing pages.

Practice Test

Unit 1 Reading
Number of Questions: 33   Number Correct _____

Unit 2 Language Arts
Number of Questions: 46   Number Correct _____

Unit 3 Mathematics
Number of Questions: 36   Number Correct _____

Unit 4 Social Studies
Number of Questions: 19   Number Correct _____

Unit 5 Science
Number of Questions: 25   Number Correct _____

Final Test

Unit 1 Reading
Number of Questions: 27   Number Correct _____

Unit 2 Language Arts
Number of Questions: 51   Number Correct _____

Unit 3 Mathematics
Number of Questions: 45   Number Correct _____

Unit 4 Social Studies
Number of Questions: 11   Number Correct _____

Unit 5 Science
Number of Questions: 13   Number Correct _____

Practice Test Answer Sheet

Fill in **only one** letter for each item. If you change an answer, make sure to erase your first mark completely.

Unit 1: Reading, pages 79–93

A Ⓐ Ⓑ Ⓒ Ⓓ   7 Ⓐ Ⓑ Ⓒ Ⓓ   15 Ⓐ Ⓑ Ⓒ Ⓓ   22 Ⓐ Ⓑ Ⓒ Ⓓ   29 Ⓐ Ⓑ Ⓒ Ⓓ

B Ⓕ Ⓖ Ⓗ Ⓙ   8 Ⓕ Ⓖ Ⓗ Ⓙ   16 Ⓕ Ⓖ Ⓗ Ⓙ   23 Ⓕ Ⓖ Ⓗ Ⓙ   30 Ⓕ Ⓖ Ⓗ Ⓙ

1 Ⓐ Ⓑ Ⓒ Ⓓ   9 Ⓐ Ⓑ Ⓒ Ⓓ   17 Ⓐ Ⓑ Ⓒ Ⓓ   24 Ⓐ Ⓑ Ⓒ Ⓓ   31 Ⓐ Ⓑ Ⓒ Ⓓ

2 Ⓕ Ⓖ Ⓗ Ⓙ   10 Ⓕ Ⓖ Ⓗ Ⓙ   18 Ⓕ Ⓖ Ⓗ Ⓙ   25 Ⓕ Ⓖ Ⓗ Ⓙ   32 Ⓕ Ⓖ Ⓗ Ⓙ

3 Ⓐ Ⓑ Ⓒ Ⓓ   11 Ⓐ Ⓑ Ⓒ Ⓓ   19 Ⓐ Ⓑ Ⓒ Ⓓ   26 Ⓐ Ⓑ Ⓒ Ⓓ   33 Ⓐ Ⓑ Ⓒ Ⓓ

4 Ⓕ Ⓖ Ⓗ Ⓙ   12 Ⓕ Ⓖ Ⓗ Ⓙ   20 Ⓕ Ⓖ Ⓗ Ⓙ   D Ⓐ Ⓑ Ⓒ Ⓓ

5 Ⓐ Ⓑ Ⓒ Ⓓ   13 Ⓐ Ⓑ Ⓒ Ⓓ   21 Ⓐ Ⓑ Ⓒ Ⓓ   27 Ⓐ Ⓑ Ⓒ Ⓓ

6 Ⓕ Ⓖ Ⓗ Ⓙ   14 Ⓕ Ⓖ Ⓗ Ⓙ   C Ⓐ Ⓑ Ⓒ Ⓓ   28 Ⓕ Ⓖ Ⓗ Ⓙ

Unit 2: Language Arts, pages 94–104

A Ⓐ Ⓑ Ⓒ Ⓓ   10 Ⓕ Ⓖ Ⓗ Ⓙ   19 Ⓐ Ⓑ Ⓒ Ⓓ   27 Ⓐ Ⓑ Ⓒ Ⓓ   38 Ⓕ Ⓖ Ⓗ Ⓙ

1 Ⓐ Ⓑ Ⓒ Ⓓ   11 Ⓐ Ⓑ Ⓒ Ⓓ   20 Ⓕ Ⓖ Ⓗ Ⓙ   28 Ⓕ Ⓖ Ⓗ Ⓙ   39 Ⓐ Ⓑ Ⓒ Ⓓ

2 Ⓕ Ⓖ Ⓗ Ⓙ   12 Ⓕ Ⓖ Ⓗ Ⓙ   21 Ⓐ Ⓑ Ⓒ Ⓓ   29 Ⓐ Ⓑ Ⓒ Ⓓ   40 Ⓕ Ⓖ Ⓗ Ⓙ

B Ⓐ Ⓑ Ⓒ Ⓓ   C Ⓐ Ⓑ Ⓒ Ⓓ   22 Ⓕ Ⓖ Ⓗ Ⓙ   30 Ⓕ Ⓖ Ⓗ Ⓙ   41 Ⓐ Ⓑ Ⓒ Ⓓ

3 Ⓐ Ⓑ Ⓒ Ⓓ   13 Ⓐ Ⓑ Ⓒ Ⓓ   E Ⓐ Ⓑ Ⓒ Ⓓ   31 Ⓐ Ⓑ Ⓒ Ⓓ   42 Ⓕ Ⓖ Ⓗ Ⓙ

4 Ⓕ Ⓖ Ⓗ Ⓙ   14 Ⓕ Ⓖ Ⓗ Ⓙ   23 Ⓐ Ⓑ Ⓒ Ⓓ   32 Ⓕ Ⓖ Ⓗ Ⓙ   H Ⓐ Ⓑ Ⓒ Ⓓ Ⓔ

5 Ⓐ Ⓑ Ⓒ Ⓓ   15 Ⓐ Ⓑ Ⓒ Ⓓ   24 Ⓕ Ⓖ Ⓗ Ⓙ   33 Ⓐ Ⓑ Ⓒ Ⓓ   43 Ⓐ Ⓑ Ⓒ Ⓓ Ⓔ

6 Ⓕ Ⓖ Ⓗ Ⓙ   16 Ⓕ Ⓖ Ⓗ Ⓙ   F Ⓐ Ⓑ Ⓒ Ⓓ Ⓔ   34 Ⓕ Ⓖ Ⓗ Ⓙ   44 Ⓕ Ⓖ Ⓗ Ⓙ Ⓚ

7 Ⓐ Ⓑ Ⓒ Ⓓ   D Ⓐ Ⓑ Ⓒ Ⓓ   25 Ⓐ Ⓑ Ⓒ Ⓓ Ⓔ   35 Ⓐ Ⓑ Ⓒ Ⓓ   45 Ⓐ Ⓑ Ⓒ Ⓓ Ⓔ

8 Ⓕ Ⓖ Ⓗ Ⓙ   17 Ⓐ Ⓑ Ⓒ Ⓓ   26 Ⓕ Ⓖ Ⓗ Ⓙ Ⓚ   36 Ⓕ Ⓖ Ⓗ Ⓙ   46 Ⓕ Ⓖ Ⓗ Ⓙ Ⓚ

9 Ⓐ Ⓑ Ⓒ Ⓓ   18 Ⓕ Ⓖ Ⓗ Ⓙ   G Ⓐ Ⓑ Ⓒ Ⓓ   37 Ⓐ Ⓑ Ⓒ Ⓓ

Practice Test Answer Sheet

Unit 3: Mathematics, pages 105–114

A Ⓐ Ⓑ Ⓒ Ⓓ Ⓔ   7 Ⓐ Ⓑ Ⓒ Ⓓ   16 Ⓕ Ⓖ Ⓗ Ⓙ   23 Ⓐ Ⓑ Ⓒ Ⓓ Ⓔ   31 Ⓐ Ⓑ Ⓒ Ⓓ

B Ⓕ Ⓖ Ⓗ Ⓙ Ⓚ   8 Ⓕ Ⓖ Ⓗ Ⓙ   17 Ⓐ Ⓑ Ⓒ Ⓓ   24 Ⓕ Ⓖ Ⓗ Ⓙ Ⓚ   32 Ⓕ Ⓖ Ⓗ Ⓙ

1 Ⓐ Ⓑ Ⓒ Ⓓ Ⓔ   9 Ⓐ Ⓑ Ⓒ Ⓓ   18 Ⓕ Ⓖ Ⓗ Ⓙ   25 Ⓐ Ⓑ Ⓒ Ⓓ Ⓔ   33 Ⓐ Ⓑ Ⓒ Ⓓ

2 Ⓕ Ⓖ Ⓗ Ⓙ Ⓚ   10 Ⓕ Ⓖ Ⓗ Ⓙ   19 Ⓐ Ⓑ Ⓒ Ⓓ   26 Ⓕ Ⓖ Ⓗ Ⓙ Ⓚ   34 Ⓕ Ⓖ Ⓗ Ⓙ

3 Ⓐ Ⓑ Ⓒ Ⓓ Ⓔ   11 Ⓐ Ⓑ Ⓒ Ⓓ   20 Ⓕ Ⓖ Ⓗ Ⓙ   F Ⓐ Ⓑ Ⓒ Ⓓ   35 Ⓐ Ⓑ Ⓒ Ⓓ

4 Ⓕ Ⓖ Ⓗ Ⓙ Ⓚ   12 Ⓕ Ⓖ Ⓗ Ⓙ   D Ⓐ Ⓑ Ⓒ Ⓓ Ⓔ   27 Ⓐ Ⓑ Ⓒ Ⓓ   36 Ⓕ Ⓖ Ⓗ Ⓙ

5 Ⓐ Ⓑ Ⓒ Ⓓ Ⓔ   13 Ⓐ Ⓑ Ⓒ Ⓓ   E Ⓕ Ⓖ Ⓗ Ⓙ Ⓚ   28 Ⓕ Ⓖ Ⓗ Ⓙ

6 Ⓕ Ⓖ Ⓗ Ⓙ Ⓚ   14 Ⓕ Ⓖ Ⓗ Ⓙ   21 Ⓐ Ⓑ Ⓒ Ⓓ Ⓔ   29 Ⓐ Ⓑ Ⓒ Ⓓ

C Ⓐ Ⓑ Ⓒ Ⓓ   15 Ⓐ Ⓑ Ⓒ Ⓓ   22 Ⓕ Ⓖ Ⓗ Ⓙ Ⓚ   30 Ⓕ Ⓖ Ⓗ Ⓙ

Unit 4: Social Studies, pages 115–118

1 Ⓐ Ⓑ Ⓒ Ⓓ   5 Ⓕ Ⓖ Ⓗ Ⓙ   9 Ⓕ Ⓖ Ⓗ Ⓙ   13 Ⓕ Ⓖ Ⓗ Ⓙ   17 Ⓕ Ⓖ Ⓗ Ⓙ

2 Ⓕ Ⓖ Ⓗ Ⓙ   6 Ⓐ Ⓑ Ⓒ Ⓓ   10 Ⓐ Ⓑ Ⓒ Ⓓ   14 Ⓐ Ⓑ Ⓒ Ⓓ   18 Ⓐ Ⓑ Ⓒ Ⓓ

3 Ⓐ Ⓑ Ⓒ Ⓓ   7 Ⓕ Ⓖ Ⓗ Ⓙ   11 Ⓕ Ⓖ Ⓗ Ⓙ   15 Ⓕ Ⓖ Ⓗ Ⓙ   19 Ⓕ Ⓖ Ⓗ Ⓙ

4 Ⓐ Ⓑ Ⓒ Ⓓ   8 Ⓐ Ⓑ Ⓒ Ⓓ   12 Ⓐ Ⓑ Ⓒ Ⓓ   16 Ⓐ Ⓑ Ⓒ Ⓓ

Unit 5: Science, pages 119–122

1 Ⓐ Ⓑ Ⓒ Ⓓ   6 Ⓕ Ⓖ Ⓗ Ⓙ   11 Ⓐ Ⓑ Ⓒ Ⓓ   16 Ⓕ Ⓖ Ⓗ Ⓙ   21 Ⓐ Ⓑ Ⓒ Ⓓ

2 Ⓕ Ⓖ Ⓗ Ⓙ   7 Ⓐ Ⓑ Ⓒ Ⓓ   12 Ⓕ Ⓖ Ⓗ Ⓙ   17 Ⓐ Ⓑ Ⓒ Ⓓ   22 Ⓕ Ⓖ Ⓗ Ⓙ

3 Ⓐ Ⓑ Ⓒ Ⓓ   8 Ⓕ Ⓖ Ⓗ Ⓙ   13 Ⓐ Ⓑ Ⓒ Ⓓ   18 Ⓕ Ⓖ Ⓗ Ⓙ   23 Ⓐ Ⓑ Ⓒ Ⓓ

4 Ⓕ Ⓖ Ⓗ Ⓙ   9 Ⓐ Ⓑ Ⓒ Ⓓ   14 Ⓕ Ⓖ Ⓗ Ⓙ   19 Ⓐ Ⓑ Ⓒ Ⓓ   24 Ⓕ Ⓖ Ⓗ Ⓙ

5 Ⓐ Ⓑ Ⓒ Ⓓ   10 Ⓕ Ⓖ Ⓗ Ⓙ   15 Ⓐ Ⓑ Ⓒ Ⓓ   20 Ⓕ Ⓖ Ⓗ Ⓙ   25 Ⓐ Ⓑ Ⓒ Ⓓ

Lesson 1 Reading Nonfiction

SAMPLE A

Do you know how television works? The picture taken by the camera is turned into an electronic pulse that is broadcast into the air. The receiver in your television picks up the signal and turns it into the picture you see on your screen.

In this passage, the word "broadcast" means

A received   C created
B sent   D weakened

SAMPLE B

Which choice best combines these sentences into one?
This gift is for my cousin.
My cousin is having a birthday soon.

F My cousin is having a birthday soon, but this gift is for her.
G My cousin, who is having a birthday soon, this gift is for.
H This gift is for my cousin, who is having a birthday soon.
J This gift, which is for my cousin having a birthday soon.

Skim the story before you answer the questions. Just try to get a general understanding of what it's about.

Skim the questions. Answer the easiest questions first.

Bigger And Better

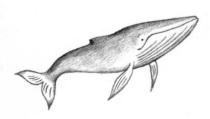

People are fascinated with making things bigger and better. Tall mountains, skyscrapers, long rivers . . . things that push the limits captivate our imaginations. In this section, you will read about some of these things and people who mastered them.

GO

Directions: The man who climbed Mt. Everest did more than just conquer a mountain. He used his fame to support causes he thought were important. Read his story, then do numbers 1–8.

CONQUERING EVEREST

When Edmund Hillary was born in New Zealand, in 1919, he had no idea he would someday be knighted by the Queen of England. Here is the story of how the young boy grew to be a great adventurer and humanitarian.

Edmund Hillary first discovered mountain climbing on a school field trip. He loved climbing right away and would climb the local mountains at every opportunity. To climb safely, a person must be strong and reliable; Edmund was both. By the time he was in his twenties, Edmund was recognized for his mountaineering talents and had mastered many difficult feats.

The young climber then decided to try some mountains in Europe. Through his adventures there, Edmund met Sir John Hunt, who was planning an expedition to Mount Everest. Situated on the border of Nepal and Tibet, the 29,028-foot high peak had never been climbed successfully. Hunt quickly invited Edmund to go along on the trip, and the result was history. On May 29, 1953, Edmund and his Nepalese guide, Tenzing Norgay, were the first people to reach the summit of the world's tallest mountain.

Now a famous adventurer, Edmund was sought after by leaders of other expeditions. Sir Vivian Fuchs asked for Edmund's help with a Trans-Antarctic project. In 1957 and 1958, Edmund was responsible for setting up supply areas around the South Pole. To do this, he drove farm tractors to the supply sites and left food and fuel behind. When he had finished

GO

the deliveries he drove all the way to the South Pole. He was the first to do so in 46 years. Edmund's skilled management of the assignment helped Fuchs's team attain its goal.

Another of Edmund's accomplishments was an expedition along the length of the Ganges River. This river, sacred to Hindu people, flows for 1560 miles in India and Pakistan. Edmund's team traveled by jet boat and on foot to the source of the Ganges in the Himalayan Mountains.

For the next twenty years Edmund continued to climb in the Himalayas. During this time, he came to know and depend on the Sherpas, the Nepalese people. Edmund's concern and appreciation for the Sherpas was so great that he raised money to build schools and hospitals for them, even helping with the construction.

Edmund's concern for people led him to contribute in other areas as well. He was an active spokesperson for many social issues, led the Volunteer Service Abroad Program, and lent his support to adventure groups. In between his many activities, Edmund wrote books about his adventures.

Because of his many accomplishments and his dedication to human and environmental rights, Edmund received several honors. He was knighted in 1953, and from then on he was called Sir Edmund Hillary. Others recognized him with honorary degrees and decorations. He even served as New Zealand's high commissioner to India in the 1980s.

Sir Edmund Hillary accomplished much in his life. He is an important figure not only because of his outdoor achievements, but also because of his dedication to the things he believed in. We cannot all climb high mountains, but we can certainly follow in this adventurer's footsteps and constantly strive to do better.

1 **This excerpt is mostly about a person who**

   A had dreams of becoming famous.

   B fought his way out of poverty.

   C was able to succeed despite many handicaps.

   D achieved greatness in several arenas.

2 **The word *decorations*, as it is used in the next-to-last paragraph, probably means**

   F ways to make a place look nice.

   G awards or honors.

   H ribbons and bows.

   J bright, shiny objects.

GO

3 **According to what you read in the passage, which of these statements would Sir Edmund Hillary probably support?**

   A We should explore nature responsibly.

   B People have the right to use nature as they wish.

   C It is more important to take than to give.

   D If you think you can't do something, don't try to do it.

4 **Who accompanied Sir Edmund Hillary on his most famous climb?**

   F Sir Vivian Fuchs

   G a Hindu guide

   H a Nepalese guide

   J no one—he did it alone

5 **Choose the sentence that best explains why Sir Edmund Hillary built schools and hospitals for the Sherpas.**

   A It was part of his job as high commissioner.

   B He wanted to prove that he could build things.

   C He wanted to do something to help them.

   D He did it so they would keep helping him.

GO

Directions: Use this web based on the passage to do numbers 6–8.

6 **This web was designed to describe Sir Edmund Hillary's**

 F many degrees and awards.

 G various outdoor adventures.

 H social and humanitarian work.

 J attributes and achievements.

7 **Choose the word that best fills Space 1.**

 A reliable

 B unpredictable

 C reckless

 D obedient

8 **Select the phrase that best fills Space 2.**

 F was a skilled climber at an early age

 G traveled to many countries around the globe

 H contributed time and energy to many causes

 J was sought after by famous adventurers

GO

Directions: This paragraph was written by a student who read about Sir Edmund Hillary. There are some mistakes in the paragraph that should be corrected.

[1] Mountain climbing can be dangerous, so even the most skilled mountain climbers need help sometimes. [2] When climbers come to Nepal, they rely on Sherpas as guides. [3] Some famous mountain climbers are women. [4] Sherpas know the Himalayan Mountains because they live in them. [5] They are accustomed to high elevations. [6] They are also accustomed to rugged conditions. [7] For the local people, working as mountain guides providing income and adventure.

9 **Choose the best way to write Sentence 2.**

A When climbers come to Nepal relying on Sherpas as guides.

B When climbers coming to Nepal rely on Sherpas as guides.

C When climbers come to Nepal they were relying on Sherpas as guides.

D Best as it is

10 **Which of these best combines Sentences 5 and 6?**

F They are accustomed to high elevations, and they are accustomed to rugged conditions.

G They are accustomed to high elevations and rugged conditions.

H Being accustomed to high elevations, they are also accustomed to rugged conditions.

J To be accustomed to high elevations, they become accustomed to rugged conditions.

11 **Select the best way to write Sentence 7.**

A For the local people, working as mountain guides provides income and adventure.

B For the local people, to work as mountain guides is to provide income and adventure.

C Income and adventure provides work for the local people as mountain guides.

D Best as it is

12 **Choose the sentence that does *not* belong in the paragraph.**

F Sentence 1

G Sentence 2

H Sentence 3

J Sentence 4

GO

84

Directions: Read this story, then do numbers 13–21.

Giant of the Forest

Every part of the country has a special tree that is native to that region. On the northwest coast of the United States, that special tree is called the redwood. These tall, reddish-brown trees grow in beautiful forests, usually near the ocean. Redwood trees need a great deal of moisture, and being near the ocean provides them with ample exposure to rain and fog.

Redwoods grow to be very old, with some living for hundreds of years. Scientists know the age of any of these trees by looking at its growth rings. If a redwood tree is cut crossways, you can see these rings. A ring is formed for each year of a tree's life. Researchers study redwood tree rings not only to learn the age of the tree, but to learn what the climate and environmental conditions were like in the forest as the tree was growing.

The biggest redwood tree on record, the Dyerville Giant, was 370 feet tall and weighed about one million pounds. A tree like that could provide enough lumber to build many houses. Redwood trees are more than just lumber sources, however. They are ecologically important, and most of them are protected in state and national parks and will not be cut down for lumber.

Redwoods exist in ecosystems that depend on the trees for survival. The branches and leaves of redwoods collect moisture that feeds the tree and sustains the forest life below it. Many different species of flowers, plants, insects, and vertebrate animals coexist with redwoods. It is not uncommon to see deer, birds, slugs, ferns, and flowers when walking through a dense redwood forest.

Unlike most other trees, redwoods are fairly resistant to insects and floods. Redwood trees are also fire-resistant to some extent, and even depend on periodic, low-intensity fires to clear away ground cover and encourage new growth. Most redwoods that die naturally die from being knocked over by high winds.

Even after a redwood tree falls, it has an important role to play in the forest. It can take hundreds of years for a dead redwood log to decompose completely. During that time, the log is home to many animals and various types of fungus. The impact these creatures have on the log helps it to break down and become part of the soil where seeds will start new life.

GO

13 **This article is mostly about**

   A how a forest grows.

   B how to identify forest plants.

   C forest animals and birds.

   D a unique kind of tree.

14 **The author says that many animals and plants "coexist with redwoods." The word** *coexist* **probably means**

   F compete for food.

   G struggle for life.

   H live together.

   J have common enemies.

15 **Choose the sentence that best supports your answer for number 14.**

   A A forest always includes animals and plants.

   B Without animals, there wouldn't be any trees.

   C There is competition between animals and plants.

   D The forest is an extremely wild place.

16 **Low-intensity forest fires help redwood forests because**

   F they scare away animals and birds.

   G the old undergrowth is burned away.

   H they help the trees to decompose faster.

   J they turn the tree bark a reddish color.

GO

Here is a chart that summarizes some of the information in the article. Use it to do numbers 17 and 18.

Redwood Trees

Characteristics You Can See	Characteristics You Can't See
reddish-brown bark	fire-resistant wood
grow tall	leaves give off moisture

17 **Choose the phrase that would probably fit under "Characteristics You Can See."**

A flood-resistant

B resistant to insects

C can be very old

D can have wide bases

18 **This chart is designed to**

F tell the main idea.

G organize information.

H put events in sequence.

J show which things are true.

19 **Select the sentence that best summarizes the life cycle of a redwood tree.**

A When a redwood tree dies, the log is always made into lumber.

B Redwoods grow, die, and decompose all within one year.

C A redwood tree dies only when it is knocked over by the wind.

D Redwood trees grow, die, then decompose into the earth.

20 **Which of these facts about the article helps identify it as a *descriptive passage?***

F It is written in question-and-answer format.

G It gives steps and teaches a new technique.

H It includes a wide range of information.

J It is about something that is found in nature.

21 **If you wanted to find out more about redwood trees, which of these resources would be most helpful?**

A an encyclopedia

B a college dictionary

C a world atlas

D a United States map

STOP

Lesson 2 Reading Fiction

Nature is more exciting than many young people think. Read this story about a boy who made this discovery for himself.

SAMPLE C

As Jane swam the last few strokes of the race, she could hardly believe she had done it. After the accident, no one thought she would ever compete again. Now she was just a second away from a state record.

Jane had probably

A always been the best swimmer on the team.

B spent a long time recovering from an injury.

C decided to give up swimming.

D taken up swimming late in life.

Read the question, look at the answer choices, then read the question again.

Think about what the author means as you read the story. This will help you answer the questions.

Directions: Read this story about a boy who found something that is more interesting than television, then do numbers 22–26.

The Big Surprise

"Lucky you," said Mrs. Barker. "We're staying up late tonight."

"Great!" cried Jeff. "That means I get to watch the game on television."

"Not really," Mrs. Barker replied. "You're going to watch something, but I think it's better than television."

"Well, what is it?" Jeff asked.

"It's a surprise," she replied. "We'll get going as soon as you help me with the dishes." And that was that. Jeff knew he would just have to wait and see.

An hour later, they were turning off the highway and taking a few different roads, each one smaller, and leading farther away from civilization. "Does anyone even live out here, Mom?" Again, his mother smiled and said nothing.

After several more minutes they pulled into a parking lot. Jeff was surprised to see some people he knew standing around and talking. "Hey, guys. Glad you could make it," said Dr. Jensen, one

GO

of his mother's friends who taught at the university.

"I still don't get it, Mom," Jeff said, his forehead wrinkled. "Why are we all out here in this dark place?"

Just then, Jeff saw that they were parked near a huge, oddly-shaped building. "It's the Banes Observatory, Jeff," his mother said. "I wanted to show you something bigger and better than television. Take a look at the sky. Now come on inside. You're going to see the sky like you've never seen it before."

The group entered the building and walked onto a platform. Jeff was still a little confused, but he was also intrigued. The inside of the building was a huge dome, and in the middle was a strange-looking device.

"This is a sixty-inch telescope," Dr. Jensen told the group. "By looking through it we can view stars, planets, and other things close up." She explained that tonight they would be looking at the planet Saturn, as well as other objects in the night sky. "Why don't you go first, Jeff?"

He hesitated for a minute because everyone was watching him. Finally, he put his face closer to the eyepiece. He looked through it with one eye and closed the other one. Through the telescope, Jeff saw a big, round, glowing planet with rings around it. Jeff had seen Saturn before, but it was just a pinpoint of light in the night sky. Now, it was hundreds of times bigger, and the rings were breathtaking. "Wow. It looks so different through the telescope," he exclaimed.

"Well," asked Mrs. Barker, holding her

son's shoulders. "Would you rather we went home to watch the big game?"

"Forget the game," Jeff replied. "This is unbelievable."

22 **Without the telescope, Saturn is a pinpoint of light in the night sky. This description in the sixth paragraph on this page means that**

A it was the brightest light in the sky.

B the details of the planet couldn't be seen.

C the planet is long and thin, like a pin.

D Saturn was being compared to something metal.

23 **When Jeff looks through an eyepiece, it probably means that he**

F gazes out a huge window.

G peers into a small, dark box.

H looks into a small, round lens.

J puts on a special pair of glasses.

24 **What reaction does Jeff have after he looks through the telescope?**

A He wishes he had stayed home to watch the game.

B He understands why his mother brought him.

C He decides that he wants a telescope of his own.

D He still doesn't understand the point of the trip.

GO

Here is a map that Jeff drew to show his friends how to get to the observatory. Use the map to do numbers 25 and 26.

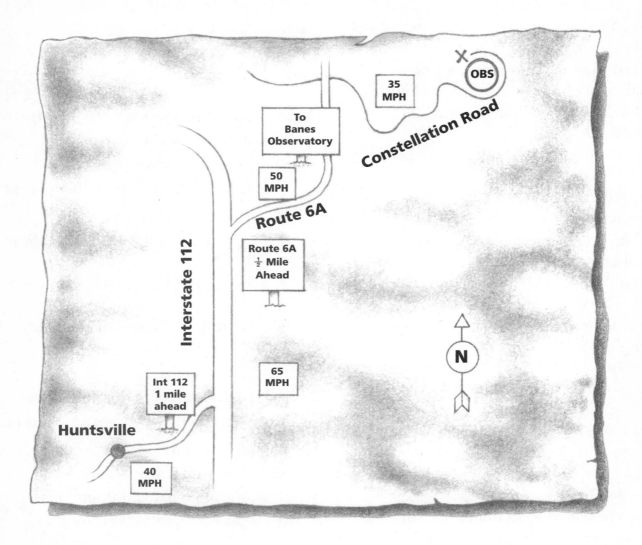

25 When people are following Jeff's map, which road are they on when they see a sign directing them to their destination?

F Huntsdale Road

G Interstate 112

H Route 6A

J Constellation Road

26 According to your answer for number 25, how fast will they be driving before they make the turn toward their destination?

A 40 miles per hour

B 65 miles per hour

C 50 miles per hour

D 35 miles per hour

STOP

Lesson 3 Review

SAMPLE D

Scientists discovering better ways to explore outer space.

Which is the best way to write the sentence above?

A Outer space is being explored better by discovering scientists.

B Exploring outer space, scientists are discovering better ways.

C Scientists are discovering better ways to explore outer space.

D Best as it is

Directions: This paragraph about observatories needs some correcting.

¹ Observatories are special places to be viewing stars, planets, and other objects in the sky. ² They are huge buildings that hold telescopes as big as houses. ³ Observatories are operated by astronomers, scientists who study our universe. ⁴ The scientists point the telescopes at objects they want to see more closely. ⁵ Observatories are usually in high places. ⁶ They are usually far from big cities. ⁷ This way, lights from civilization will not interfere with the view of the night sky.

27 **Select the best way to write Sentence 1.**

A Observatories are special places for planets, and other objects in the sky to view.

B Observatories are special places to view stars, planets, and other objects in the sky.

C Stars, planets, and other objects in the sky being viewed, there are observatories.

D Best as it is

GO

28 **Where would this sentence best fit in the passage?**

Although it can take time to get to an observatory, the view you will find there is worth the trip.

F after Sentence 2
G after Sentence 3
H after Sentence 5
J after Sentence 7

29 **Which of these shows the best way to write Sentence 4?**

A Point the telescopes at objects, the scientists want to see them more closely.
B The scientists will point the telescopes at objects they will be wanting to see more closely.
C The scientists, who point the telescopes at objects, closely want to see.
D Best as it is

30 **Which of these best combines Sentences 5 and 6 into one sentence?**

F Observatories are usually far from big cities in high places.
G Observatories are usually in high places, and observatories are usually far from big cities.
H Usually in high places, observatories are usually far from big cities.
J Best as it is

GO

31 **Choose the sentence that best supports this topic sentence.**

French undersea explorer Jacques Cousteau, who is well-known for his television specials, is also an inventor.

A In recent years, scientists have become more interested in the oceans and seas.

B Cousteau contributed to the creation of an undersea diving saucer and the first deep-water diving suit.

C Explorers like Cousteau have an exciting life, but it also includes lots of hard work.

D Inventors like Cousteau contribute to improving our lives in many important ways.

32 **Choose the sentence that best supports this topic sentence.**

Margaret Bourke-White was an American photographer who recorded images of our country's industrial and architectural progress.

F One of her most famous photographs shows the gigantic Hoover Dam under construction.

G Magazines buy pictures taken by photographers, especially those who are famous.

H Some photographers work for newspapers and magazines, and others work independently.

J She served as a war correspondent during World War II.

33 **Choose the sentence that best combines the two sentences into one.**

Quartz is one kind of semi-precious stone.
Jade is another kind of semi-precious stone.

A Quartz is one kind of semi-precious stone, or there is also another kind, jade.

B Quartz, one kind of semi-precious stone, with another kind being jade.

C Quartz and jade being two kinds of semi-precious stones.

D Quartz is one kind of semi-precious stone, and jade is another.

STOP

Language Arts

Lesson 1 Vocabulary

Directions: For Sample A and numbers 1 and 2, read the sentences. Choose the word that correctly completes **both** sentences.

SAMPLE A

Tim seems to have good _____.

Birds can _____ a storm.

A judgment
B feel
C sense
D reasoning

1 This _____ is American history.

The _____ of the river has changed.

A class   **C** depth
B path   **D** course

2 Soup is cooking on the _____.

Out West, cattle roam the open _____.

F range   **H** prairie
G stove   **J** plains

Directions: For Sample B and numbers 3 and 4, choose the word that means the **opposite** of the underlined word.

SAMPLE B

inevitable situation

A avoidable
B confusing
C stressful
D enjoyable

3 ignite a fire

A light
B approach
C extinguish
D observe

4 feel enmity

F disappointment
G friendship
H impatience
J relief

Stay with your first answer. Change it only if you are sure another one is better.

Use the meaning of a sentence or phrase to find the right answer.

GO

Directions: For numbers 5–8, choose the word that means the same, or about the same, as the underlined word.

5 <u>absurd</u> idea

   A unusual   **C** agreeable

   B clever   **D** ridiculous

7 <u>detach</u> a wire

   A insulate   **C** disconnect

   B attach   **D** ridiculous

6 surprising <u>verdict</u>

   F question   **H** investment

   G decision   **J** vacation

8 <u>lofty</u> expectations

   F high   **H** curious

   G minimal   **J** impossible

Directions: For numbers 9–12, read the paragraph. For each numbered blank, there is a list of words with the same number. Choose the word from each list that best completes the meaning of the paragraph.

Millions of people each year __(9)__ a small business. Often, they __(10)__ the business with their savings or money they have borrowed from family members. With a little luck and __(11)__ effort, these businesses succeed and grow. Once they __(12)__ , these businesses create useful products and services, as well as provide jobs.

9 **A** replenish   **C** cook

     B criticize   **D** establish

11 **A** trivial   **C** considerable

      B meaningless **D** comical

10 **F** finance   **H** align

      G terminate   **J** separate

12 **F** terminate   **H** dissolve

      G mature   **J** deteriorate

STOP

Lesson 2 Language Mechanics

Directions: For Sample C and numbers 13–16, look at the underlined part of the sentence. Choose the answer that shows the best capitalization and punctuation for that part.

SAMPLE C

Is this your <u>book, Nikki?</u>

A book; Nikki?
B book: Nikki?
C book Nikki?
D Correct as it is

13 **Sadie, my brother's <u>beagle, is</u> black and tan with droopy ears.**

A beagle; is
B beagle: is
C beagle is
D Correct as it is

14 **"Without the sun, no life could exist on <u>earth" insisted</u> Mr. Johnston.**

F earth, insisted
G earth," insisted
H earth insisted
J Correct as it is

15 **Greg <u>asked "Has</u> anybody seen the movie playing at the Oak Ridge Cinema?"**

A asked, "Has
B asked "has
C asked has
D Correct as it is

16 **<u>Iv'e heard</u> there are many bears in Montana.**

F Ive heard
G Ive' heard
H I've heard
J Correct as it is

Directions: For Sample D and numbers 17 and 18, find the sentence that is written correctly and shows the correct capitalization and punctuation.

SAMPLE D

A The saxophone; so I hear is difficult to play.
B Big band music, says my dad is fun to dance to.
C No, I don't know how to play the piano.
D Yes there are many great jazz musicians in New York?

TIPS Look for capitalization mistakes first, then look for punctuation errors.

Don't choose "Correct as it is" too often.

GO

17 **A** The boy ran after him shouting, "you dropped your map."

B "After the museum, let's have some lunch, suggested Paul."

C "Look how beautiful these marble statues are!" exclaimed Anna.

D Samuel inquired, "Would you tell me how to find the museum"?

18 **F** Having grown up in the Midwest; Marta is used to the snow.

G Since it rains almost everyday. I always carry an umbrella.

H Being a pilot, Constance, knows how to read the weather.

J Because we watch the weather forecast, we are always prepared.

Directions: For numbers 19–22, read the letter and the underlined parts. Choose the answer that shows the best capitalization and punctuation for each part.

(19)   I just received a letter from my new pen pal Celine, she

lives on an island called Martinique in the Caribbean Sea. In her

(20)   letter, she wrote, that Martinique is very beautiful and has sandy

(21)   beaches, high mountains, and lots of flowers. She goes to the

(22)   beach almost every day and swims in the clear Blue Sea.

19 **A** Celine? She
    B Celine, she
    C Celine. She
    D Correct as it is

21 **A** beaches, high, mountains, and
    B beaches high mountains, and
    C beaches high mountains and
    D Correct as it is

20 **F** wrote, That
    G wrote that
    H wrote, "That
    J Correct as it is

22 **F** clear, blue sea
    G Clear Blue Sea
    H clear blue, Sea
    J Correct as it is

STOP

Lesson 3 Spelling

Directions: For Sample E and numbers 23 and 24, choose the word that is spelled correctly and best completes the sentence.

SAMPLE E

I had a chance to _____ when we were on vacation.

A snorkle   **C** snorlkel

B snorkel   **D** snoarke

23 A _____ passed near our town.

A syclone

B sycloan

C cyclone

D cycloan

24 My parents hired a _____ to add a room to our house.

F carpentar

G carpentre

H carpentir

J carpenter

Directions: For Sample F and numbers 25 and 26, read each phrase. Find the underlined word that is **not** spelled correctly. If all the underlined words are spelled correctly, mark "All correct."

SAMPLE F

A good possibility

B car accessories

C assemble parts

D irrigate a field

E All correct

25 **A** her preference

B good deal

C dependible friend

D kilogram of flour

E All correct

26 **F** organize a meeting

G act neglagent

H newspaper story

J contrary opinion

K All correct

Don't spend too much time looking at the words. Pretty soon, they all begin to look like they are spelled wrong.

Use a system when you look for errors. Look at the beginning of the word first, then the middle, then the end. The final step is to look at the whole word while you say it to yourself.

STOP

Lesson 4 Writing

Directions: Read the short story. Then write a few sentences to answer each question.

"I'm starving," Kelly said to Sheila as the girls walked home from school.

Sheila rolled her eyes. "You're always starving," she said. "We'll have something when we get to my house."

Kelly walked slightly behind Sheila. Sheila always walked so fast. Her long, beautiful hair went "swoosh, swoosh" with every step. And Sheila always looked perfect in her coordinated outfits.

No one was home when they got to Sheila's house. No one ever seemed to be home at Sheila's house. Kelly had two younger brothers and an older sister. "It must be so amazing to have the whole house to yourself. I'm lucky if I can be alone for five minutes," Kelly said.

"Yeah, it's awesome," said Sheila. "I can pretty much do whatever I want. Do you want to order a pizza? There's nothing in the refrigerator."

"That's OK," said Kelly. There was never anything in Sheila's refrigerator. "I have to be home for dinner soon."

Sheila rolled her eyes again. "I would go crazy if people told me what to do all the time."

"Well, you're lucky," said Kelly. Sheila was lucky. She had perfect hair, perfect clothes, a big, perfect house— a perfect life. "I would give anything to be Sheila for just one day," Kelly often thought.

Just then, the phone rang. "Hi, mom," she heard Sheila say. "No, it's OK. It's fine, I understand." She hung up. "My mom's having dinner out again," she said. "Are you sure you can't stay for pizza?"

"Sorry. I really have to go," said Kelly. "Whatever. See you."

Kelly saw Sheila looking out the window as she turned down the street. Suddenly Sheila's house looked very big, and Sheila looked very small.

How do the characters feel about each other? _____

_____

_____

_____

Do Kelly's feelings change by the end of the story? Explain. _____

_____

_____

_____

GO

Practice Test
Language Arts

Directions: Should everyone get a college education?
Write four or five paragraphs explaining your opinion.

_____

_____

_____

_____

_____

_____

_____

_____

_____

_____

_____

_____

_____

_____

_____

_____

_____

_____

STOP

Lesson 5 Review

Directions: For Sample G and numbers 27–29, read the sentences. Choose the word that correctly completes **both** sentences.

SAMPLE G

The insurance _____ is affordable.

Our _____ is to accept all returns.

A plan
B procedure
C guarantee
D policy

27 This _____ leads to the basement.

Read the _____ about Asia.

A hallway
B paragraph
C passage
D stair

28 This switch _____ the motor.

Mrs. Palmer _____ two companies.

F starts
G manages
H owns
J controls

29 The _____ wanted better wages.

The countries formed a _____.

A union
B workers
C bond
D employees

Directions: For numbers 30 and 31, choose the word that means the **opposite** of the underlined word.

30 <u>massive</u> storm
F enormous
G small
H unexpected
J predicted

31 <u>reckless</u> action
A cautious
B thoughtless
C planned
D responsible

Directions: For number 32, choose the word that means the same, or about the same, as the underlined word.

32 temperature <u>fluctuated</u>
F stabilized
G deteriorated
H initiated
J varied

GO

Directions: For numbers 33 and 34, choose the answer that is written correctly and shows the best capitalization and punctuation.

33
A Stuart said in disbelief, "he is juggling eight flaming swords."

B "I wonder," puzzled Rose, "Why he doesnt fall from the highwire."

C Mark said, "They must have trained for years to be so good."

D "Watching the trapeze artists, said Rachel, makes me nervous."

34
F The meeting; will be on Tuesday.

G Gina is president. Until the next election.

H Everyone, at the meeting, is a member.

J If you are late, we'll start without you.

Directions: For numbers 35–38, read the paragraph and the underlined parts. Choose the answer that shows the best capitalization and punctuation for each part.

Director of Subscription Services October 23, 2001
Hikers & Campers
(35) p.o. box 2326
(36) Chicago, Illinois, 60613

Dear Director:
  I have not received the last two issues of *Hikers & Campers* magazine. I request
(37) that you extend my current subscription, for two months to make up for the two issues I missed. I would appreciate your help in solving this problem.
(38)   sincerely:
            Tomas Fisher

35
A P.O. Box, 2326
B P.O. box 2326
C P.O. Box 2326
D Correct as it is

36
F Chicago, Illinois 60613
G Chicago Illinois 60613
H Chicago Illinois, 60613
J Correct as it is

37
A current, subscription
B current, subscription,
C current subscription
D Correct as it is

38
F Sincerely,
G sincerely;
H Sincerely
J Correct as it is

GO

Directions: For numbers 39–42, choose the word that is spelled correctly and best completes the sentence.

39 **This is a wonderful _____ story.**
   A mystary
   B mystery
   C mystury
   D mysterie

40 **Our school received good _____.**
   F publisity
   G publicitie
   H publiscity
   J publicity

41 **They _____ to ride the bus.**
   A prefered
   B prefferred
   C preferred
   D preferd

42 **The _____ was final.**
   F decision
   G desision
   H dicision
   J decisiun

Directions: For Sample H and numbers 43–46, find the underlined word that is **not** spelled correctly. If all the underlined words are spelled correctly, mark "All correct."

SAMPLE H
   A partial answer
   B two options
   C resistance to change
   D seem disrespectful
   E All correct

43 **A** city ordinance
   B paralel lines
   C chronic pain
   D relevant information
   E All correct

44 **F** prudent action
   G immediate availability
   H mandatory meeting
   J double jeopredy
   K All correct

45 **A** temperery worker
   B memorize a poem
   C small annoyance
   D aversion to spiders
   E All correct

46 **F** new bandage
   G pack equipment
   H actively participate
   J universally accepted
   K All correct

GO

Directions: Choose a career you would like to have as an adult. Write a letter to a prospective employer convincing him/her that you would be the best person for the job.

_____

_____

_____

_____

_____

_____

_____

_____

_____

_____

_____

_____

_____

_____

_____

_____

_____

_____

_____

STOP

Lesson 1 Computation

SAMPLE A

$4(5-1) =$

A 19
B 24
C 16
D 21
E None of these

SAMPLE B

$20 + {}^-15 =$

F $^-35$
G $^-5$
H 35
J 15
K None of these

1

$^-40 \times {}^-7 =$

A $^-280$
B 280
C $^-47$
D 47
E None of these

4

$12\frac{3}{4} - \frac{7}{8} =$

F $11\frac{7}{8}$
G $12\frac{7}{8}$
H $12\frac{1}{8}$
J $11\frac{5}{8}$
K None of these

2

$2\frac{1}{4}$
$+5\frac{4}{5}$

F 8
G $8\frac{1}{5}$
H $8\frac{1}{20}$
J $7\frac{1}{4}$
K None of these

5

20% of $\square = 60$

A 2400
B 300
C 240
D 3
E None of these

3

$0.054 \div 9 =$

A 0.0006
B 0.006
C 0.06
D 0.6
E None of these

6

$[(6 \times 6) + 4] \div 10 + 10 =$

F 2
G 70
H 3
J 16
K None of these

STOP

Lesson 2 | Mathematics Skills

SAMPLE
C

Susan is solving some math problems on scratch paper. Which of these statements could explain her mistake in converting centimeters to meters?

Name: _Susan_

160 centimeters = _16,000_ meters

1200 millimeters = _____ centimeters

A She multiplied instead of dividing.

B She added instead of subtracting.

C She thought that 10 millimeters are equal to 100 centimeters.

D She divided instead of multiplying.

TIPS

Read the question and look at the answer choices. Are there any you can eliminate because they can't be right?

Look for key words, numbers, and pictures in an item. Think about them and try to simplify the question so it's easier to understand.

If you aren't sure which answer is correct, take your best guess.

GO

The Historical Society

Directions: Shanna works at the Irvington Historical Society after school and on Sundays. Do numbers 7–12 about the Society.

7 Shanna worked 8 hours on Sunday and was paid $52.00. How much will she be paid for working 10 hours at the same rate?

   A $60.00   **B** $66.50   **C** $65.00   **D** $62.40

8 One of the exhibits at the museum shows an old piece of farm machinery. Two gears from the machine are shown below. Which statement is true about these two gears?

  F The small gear turns twice every time the large gear turns once.

  G The two gears turn at the same rate.

  H The small gear turns once every time the large gear turns twice.

  J The small gear turns 50 times every time the large gear turns once.

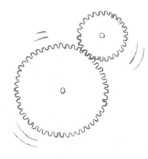

9 In 1886, there were 20 workers at a certain mill. Then the size of the work force increased by 10 people each year from 1887 to 1891. Which line on the graph correctly reflects this information?

  A P

  B Q

  C R

  D S

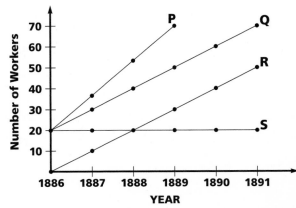

GO

10 The sketch is a model of an old manufacturing plant.

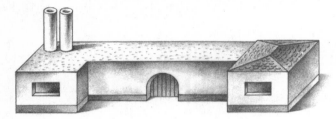

Which of these most likely shows an aerial view of the same building?

F

H

G

J

11 In one exhibit, water flows from a tank that is in the shape of a rectangular prism to a cylindrical tank. What is the minimum volume the cylindrical tank can have to hold all the water from the first tank?

A 100 cubic feet
B 50 cubic feet
C 60 cubic feet
D 75 cubic feet

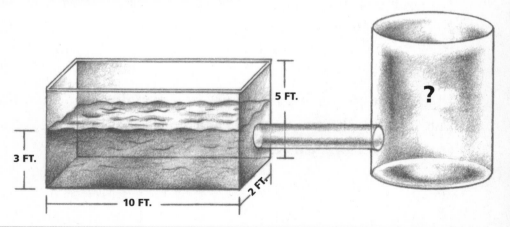

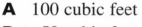

12 A school class of 13 girls and 12 boys is visiting one room of the Historical Society. If a boy walks out first, what is the probability that a girl will walk out next?

F $\frac{12}{24}$ **G** $\frac{13}{25}$ **H** $\frac{24}{25}$ **J** $\frac{13}{24}$

GO

13 If $y = {}^-4$, in which of these equations does $x = 10$?

A $x - y = 14$

B $x + y = 14$

C $x + y = {}^-6$

D $x - y = 6$

14 The table shows the weights of five different students. How many of these students weigh less than the average weight for this group?

Name	Weight
Troy	74
Lizzie	67
Anthony	95
Wai	72
Juan	76

F 1

G 2

H 3

J 4

15 Which of these is closest to the length of a paper clip?

A 3 millimeters

B 3 centimeters

C 3 meters

D 3 kilometers

16 Which of these numbers goes in the box to make the number sentence true?

$$8 + \square > 19$$

F 4

G 7

H 10

J 13

17 Which of these is another way to write 6^3?

A 3×6

B $6 + 6 + 6$

C $6 \times 6 \times 6$

D $3 \times 3 \times 3 \times 3 \times 3 \times 3$

18 If $p = 5$ and $q = 1$, what is the value of this expression?

$$3(4p - 2q) + 12$$

F 66

G 42

H $^-6$

J 30

GO

19 This computer squares numbers. Michelle put some numbers into the computer. Which of the tables below could show her results?

A

Before	After
0	0
25	5
36	6

C

Before	After
0	5
8	13
11	16

B

Before	After
1	1
4	16
8	64

D

Before	After
6	12
8	16
9	18

20 Point P is between Point Y and Point Z. Which of these does *not* contain Point P?

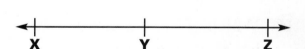

F $\overrightarrow{XZ}$

H $\overline{ZX}$

G $\overline{XZ}$

J $\overleftarrow{YX}$

STOP

Lesson 3 | Review

SAMPLE D

10% of $47.00 =

A $4.70
B $0.37
C $0.47
D $3.70
E None of these

SAMPLE E

82 ÷ 4 =

F 4
G 64
H 12
J 16
K None of these

21

$$3807.60$$
$$-\quad 0.23$$

A 3807.33
B 3807.4
C 3807.43
D 3807.77
E None of these

24

⁻30 × ⁻9 =

F ⁻270
G 270
H 39
J ⁻39
K None of these

22

85% of □ = 68

F 8.0
G 0.80
H 60.0
J 800.0
K None of these

25

3.05 ÷ 0.61 =

A 0.5
B 0.55
C 5
D 50
E None of these

23

$$2\tfrac{1}{3}$$
$$4\tfrac{1}{6}$$
$$+5\tfrac{1}{4}$$

A 12
B 11½
C 11¾
D 12¾
E None of these

26

[5 + (3 × 5)] ÷ 2 =

F 4
G 20
H 8
J 10
K None of these

GO

UNIT 3

UNIT 3

SAMPLE F

Which group of integers is in order from greatest to least?

A 6, ⁻5, 4, ⁻3, 1

B 2, 1, 0, ⁻2, ⁻1

C 8, 4, 2, ⁻2, ⁻4

D 7, 3, 0, ⁻7, ⁻3

Directions: For numbers 27–30 you do not need to calculate exact answers.
Use estimation to choose the best answer.

27 Which of these is the best estimate of 48% of 5200?

   A 1000

   B 1500

   C 2000

   D 2500

28 Rachel earns $18 a week baby-sitting. She is going to buy her brother's television set for $200. Rachel will pay her brother $12 each week. About how many months will it take her to pay for the television?

   F 4 months

   G 7 months

   H 9 months

   J 12 months

29 Which of these is the best estimate of the square root of 11?

   A less than 3

   B between 3 and 3.5

   C between 3.5 and 4

   D greater than 4

30 Which of these is the best estimate of $\frac{51}{76} \div \frac{17}{77} = \square$?

   F 3

   G 1

   H $\frac{1}{3}$

   J $\frac{1}{7}$

GO

31 Read the problem in the box and think about how you would solve it. You do not have to solve it.

> Helene bought a dozen bagels at $0.45 each and 3 scones at $1.25 each. How much did she spend?

Which of these problems would you solve the same way?

A John had $1800.00 in the bank. He bought a stereo system for $1050.00 and a printer for $249.99. How much money does he have left?

B Jennifer has 5 rings and 2 bracelets. How many pieces of jewelry does she have all together?

C Sari had 10 pieces of candy. She gave 3 pieces to Lance and 4 pieces to Dominick. How many pieces of candy does she have left?

D Homer bought 3 cans of tennis balls at $2.29 each and a tennis racquet for $129.00. How much did he spend?

32 If Point P and Point Q are two vertices of a right triangle, which of these could be the coordinates of the missing vertex?

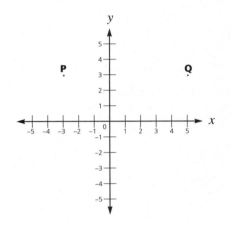

F (4, ⁻1) **H** (⁻4, ⁻1)
G (0, 0) **J** (⁻3, ⁻1)

33 This cone will be sliced as shown.

What will be the shape of the new face?

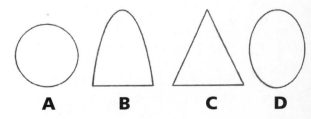

A **B** **C** **D**

34 Point R is the center of the circle. Which of these is a true statement?

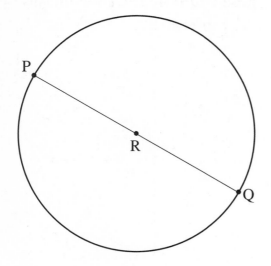

F $\overline{QR}$ is a diameter of the circle.

G $\overline{QR}$ is a radius of the circle.

H $\overline{QR}$ is the area of the circle.

J $\overline{QR}$ is the circumference of the circle.

35 Ricky needs 2 liters of salad dressing for a dinner party. The salad dressing is sold in 250-milliliter bottles that cost $2.29 each. How much money will Ricky pay for 2 liters?

A $9.16

B $18.32

C $4.29

D $22.90

36 Which of these flags would not look exactly the same after being rotated 180 degrees about its center?

F

G

H

J

STOP

114

Lesson 1 Map Skills

Directions: Study the U.S. map, then do numbers 1–3.

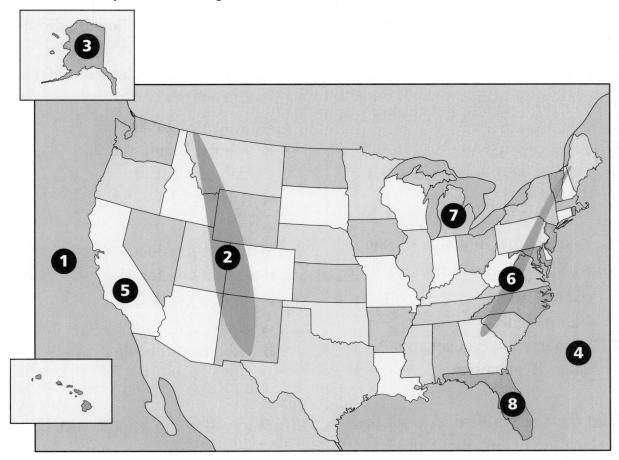

1 **What is the feature labeled 1 on the map?**

   A Atlantic Ocean   **C** Pacific Ocean

   B Gulf of Mexico   **D** Lake Superior

2 **What is the feature labeled 4 on the map?**

   F Atlantic Ocean   **H** Pacific Ocean

   G Gulf of Mexico   **J** Lake Superior

3 **What is the feature labeled 5 on the map?**

   A Arizona   **C** Wyoming

   B California   **D** Texas

STOP

Lesson 2 Social Studies Knowledge

Directions: For numbers 4–11, choose the correct answer.

4 Which of the following is *not* addressed in the first ten amendments to the Constitution?

A freedom of speech

B right to bear arms

C abolition of slavery

D right against unreasonable search and seizure

5 The first ten amendments to the United States Constitution form the

F Magna Carta.

G Bill of Rights.

H Emancipation Proclamation.

J States' Regulations.

6 Who was the major drafter of the Declaration of Independence?

A Thomas Jefferson

B Benjamin Franklin

C John Hancock

D John Adams

7 The Declaration of Independence was signed in Philadelphia. This location could best be described as

F north of Maine.

G east of the Mississippi River.

H west of Wyoming.

J south of Louisiana.

8 Who among the following did not participate in the drafting or signing of the Declaration of Independence?

A Roger Sherman

B Robert Livingston

C James Madison

D Grover Cleveland

9 Who was president of the United States during the War of 1812?

F James Madison

G George Washington

H Abraham Lincoln

J John Hancock

10 The goal of the Abolitionist Movement was

A to end slavery.

B to promote agricultural progress.

C to slow down industry.

D to influence the Continental Congress.

11 Which body of water is nearest Louisiana?

F Atlantic Ocean

G Pacific Ocean

H Gulf of Mexico

J Bering Sea

STOP

Lesson 3 Review

Directions: Study the time line that shows important events leading up to the American Revolution. Then do numbers 12–16.

Events Leading to the American Revolution

Parliament passes the Stamp Act, which meets with the cry: "Taxation without representation!"

The Townshend Acts are passed.

The Boston Massacre occurs.

People protest during the Boston Tea Party.

The Intolerable Acts are passed to punish the colonies.

Delegates from almost all colonies meet at Continental Congress and boycott all goods from England.

Delegates advise Bostonians not to honor the Intolerable Acts.

| 1765 | 1767 | 1770 | 1773 | 1774 |

12 **When does the time line show that people cried, "Taxation without representation!"**

A after the Boston Massacre

B during the Continental Congress

C after the Stamp Act was passed

D during the fifth decade of the 1700s

13 **Of all the events listed, these events occurred closest together in time.**

F Townshend Acts; boycott of English goods

G advice not to honor the Intolerable Acts; Stamp Act

H passage of the Intolerable Acts; Boston Tea Party

J Stamp Act; Townshend Acts

14 **Which of these events happened *first?***

A Boston Tea Party

B Townshend Acts

C Boston Massacre

D Stamp Act

15 **What period of time does this time line cover?**

F slightly less than one decade

G slightly more than one decade

H approximately one century

J about one millennium

16 **Which of the following events happened *last?***

A The Stamp Act was passed.

B The Intolerable Acts were passed.

C The Boston Massacre occurred.

D People protested during the Boston Tea Party.

GO

Directions: For numbers 17–19, read the passage and answer the questions that follow.

Civil War Causes

It is widely held that slavery was the cause of the U.S. Civil War, though some have put forth the theory that the economic disparity between the North and South may have also been a cause.

Some experts say that a major cause of the Civil War was political action. Their theory states that political candidates seeking election used the issue of slavery to stir up political sentiment and catapult themselves into office.

Many experts believe that a mixture of causes brought about the Civil War. It is clear that the South's economy focused on agriculture, while the North was racing along with an eye on industrialization. This difference certainly could have contributed to the causes of the Civil War, but it is certainly not the only cause. Many in the South were interested in industrialization, while many in the North owned farms.

In the final analysis, many historians believe that not only slavery, but on a deeper level, the issues that led to differences of opinion about slavery, also caused the Civil War.

17 **Which of the following is not mentioned in the passage as a cause of the Civil War?**

F stirring up political sentiment

G slavery

H arguments over weapons

J industrialization interests versus agricultural interests

18 **Who was most interested in industrialization?**

A politicians

B the North

C slaves

D the South

19 **Which is the best summary of the passage?**

F It is clear that the primary cause of the Civil War was the economic disparity between the North and South.

G While there have been many causes of the Civil War discussed, most would probably agree that slavery and opinions related to slavery were major causes.

H Industrialization and agriculture were the major contributors to the Civil War.

J Experts are evenly split as to the cause of the Civil War.

STOP

Lesson 1   Science Knowledge

Directions: For numbers 1–8, choose the correct answer.

1 Kyla's frozen pop has turned into liquid. The frozen pop has reached its

  A freezing point.
  B melting point.
  C point of no return.
  D boiling point.

2 Through his telescope, Oscar spies a heavenly body with a long tail of light. Oscar is looking at

  F an asteroid.
  G the moon.
  H a comet.
  J a speck on the lens of his telescope.

3 Hydrogen, helium, and oxygen are all

  A elements.
  B atomic weights.
  C protons.
  D neutrons.

4 The outside of a cell is called

  F the membrane.
  G the nucleus.
  H the cytoplasm.
  J the chloroplast.

5 The furthest planet from the sun is

  A Mercury.
  B Saturn.
  C Pluto.
  D Uranus.

6 Sita boils a kettle of water. Some of the water has turned into steam. Sita's water has undergone a

  F chemical change.
  G melting point.
  H change of scenery.
  J physical change.

7 A particle with a negative charge is called

  A a proton.
  B an electron.
  C a neutron.
  D a molecule.

8 Which instrument would help you calculate the velocity of a human?

  F a thermometer
  G a microscope
  H a barometer
  J a stopwatch

GO

Directions: For numbers 9–16, choose the correct answer.

9 **Which of the following is *not* a satellite?**

 A a planet
 B the sun
 C a moon
 D a comet

10 **Which of the following would you *not* find in an atom?**

 F protons
 G cytoplasm
 H neutrons
 J nucleus

11 **CO_2 is composed of what elements?**

 A calcium and oxygen
 B carbon
 C carbon and oxygen
 D carbon dioxide

12 **The closest planet to the sun is**

 F Mars.
 G Earth.
 H Venus.
 J Mercury.

13 **When in outer space, an astronaut floats because the pull of Earth's _____ is weaker.**

 A attraction
 B velocity
 C weight
 D gravity

14 **The most abundant element on Earth is**

 F oxygen.
 G nitrogen.
 H hydrogen.
 J carbon.

15 **Fe is the symbol of what element?**

 A tin
 B fluorine
 C iron
 D fermium

16 **Astronomer is to comet as botanist is to _____.**

 F geode
 G human
 H fossil
 J plant

STOP

Lesson 2 Review

Directions: For numbers 17–19, use the passage to choose the correct answer.

MELINA'S EXPERIMENT

Melina did an experiment to see how acid rain effects the growth of plants. She bought three healthy ferns and made charts to monitor the growth of each plant.

Melina watered Plant A with spring water. Plant B was watered with rain that she had collected. She watered Plant C with a mixture of spring water and lemon juice, which is acidic.

Every couple of days, Melina measured and charted the growth of each of the three plants. At the end of the month, she reviewed her results. Plant A had grown twice as much as Plant C. Plant B had grown more than Plant C, but less than Plant A.

17 **Which of the following was not a constant in Melina's experiment?**

  A the plants

  B the liquid that Melina used to water the plants

  C the amount of sunlight that each plant received

  D the soil

18 **What conclusion can be drawn about the rainwater Melina collected?**

  F The rainwater is more acidic than the mixture of lemon juice and water.

  G The rainwater is more acidic than lemon juice.

  H The rainwater is less acidic than the purified spring water.

  J The rainwater is more acidic than the purified spring water.

19 **Melina used charts to organize her**

  A data.

  B conclusions.

  C hypothesis.

  D cells.

GO

Directions: For numbers 20–25, choose the correct answer.

20 Which of the following would you do first if you wanted to set up your own science experiment?

F gather the necessary materials

G make a hypothesis

H examine your data

J predict what will happen in the experiment

21 You decide to measure how the volume of a sample of salt water changes over time. You will use a _____ to measure the change in volume.

A digital scale

B beaker

C tape measure

D graduated cylinder

22 You will leave the salt water sample in an open container, at room temperature, for several days. You suspect that some of the water from the mixture will

F crystallize.

G expand.

H condense.

J evaporate.

23 The best way to keep track of the change in volume is to

A record the volume each day and enter your data on a bar graph.

B record the volume each day and develop a prediction about how the volume will change.

C calculate how long it will take for all the water to disappear.

D record the volume each day and enter your data on a pie chart.

24 At the end of the experiment, you see that the volume of the salt water has decreased. The law of conservation of matter helps you to conclude that

F some of the water disappeared forever.

G the "missing" water has not really disappeared, but it has changed form.

H the salt has absorbed the water.

J salt water has a much lower freezing point than fresh water.

25 In this experiment, the salt water is an example of

A a solute.

B a compound.

C an element.

D a mixture.

STOP

Final Test Answer Sheet

Fill in **only one** letter for each item. If you change an answer, make sure to erase your first mark completely.

Unit 1: Reading, pages 125–130

A Ⓐ Ⓑ Ⓒ Ⓓ	**6** Ⓕ Ⓖ Ⓗ Ⓙ	**12** Ⓕ Ⓖ Ⓗ Ⓙ	**18** Ⓕ Ⓖ Ⓗ Ⓙ	**24** Ⓕ Ⓖ Ⓗ Ⓙ
1 Ⓐ Ⓑ Ⓒ Ⓓ	**7** Ⓐ Ⓑ Ⓒ Ⓓ	**13** Ⓐ Ⓑ Ⓒ Ⓓ	**19** Ⓕ Ⓖ Ⓗ Ⓙ	**25** Ⓕ Ⓖ Ⓗ Ⓙ
2 Ⓕ Ⓖ Ⓗ Ⓙ	**8** Ⓕ Ⓖ Ⓗ Ⓙ	**14** Ⓕ Ⓖ Ⓗ Ⓙ	**20** Ⓐ Ⓑ Ⓒ Ⓓ	**26** Ⓕ Ⓖ Ⓗ Ⓙ
3 Ⓐ Ⓑ Ⓒ Ⓓ	**9** Ⓐ Ⓑ Ⓒ Ⓓ	**15** Ⓐ Ⓑ Ⓒ Ⓓ	**21** Ⓐ Ⓑ Ⓒ Ⓓ	**27** Ⓕ Ⓖ Ⓗ Ⓙ
4 Ⓕ Ⓖ Ⓗ Ⓙ	**10** Ⓕ Ⓖ Ⓗ Ⓙ	**16** Ⓕ Ⓖ Ⓗ Ⓙ	**22** Ⓐ Ⓑ Ⓒ Ⓓ	
5 Ⓐ Ⓑ Ⓒ Ⓓ	**11** Ⓐ Ⓑ Ⓒ Ⓓ	**17** Ⓕ Ⓖ Ⓗ Ⓙ	**23** Ⓐ Ⓑ Ⓒ Ⓓ	

Unit 2: Language Arts, pages 131–139

A Ⓐ Ⓑ Ⓒ Ⓓ	**11** Ⓐ Ⓑ Ⓒ Ⓓ	**21** Ⓐ Ⓑ Ⓒ Ⓓ	**32** Ⓕ Ⓖ Ⓗ Ⓙ	**43** Ⓐ Ⓑ Ⓒ Ⓓ
1 Ⓐ Ⓑ Ⓒ Ⓓ	**12** Ⓕ Ⓖ Ⓗ Ⓙ	**22** Ⓕ Ⓖ Ⓗ Ⓙ	**33** Ⓐ Ⓑ Ⓒ Ⓓ	**44** Ⓕ Ⓖ Ⓗ Ⓙ
2 Ⓕ Ⓖ Ⓗ Ⓙ	**B** Ⓐ Ⓑ Ⓒ Ⓓ	**23** Ⓐ Ⓑ Ⓒ Ⓓ	**34** Ⓕ Ⓖ Ⓗ Ⓙ	**45** Ⓐ Ⓑ Ⓒ Ⓓ
3 Ⓐ Ⓑ Ⓒ Ⓓ	**13** Ⓐ Ⓑ Ⓒ Ⓓ	**24** Ⓕ Ⓖ Ⓗ Ⓙ	**35** Ⓐ Ⓑ Ⓒ Ⓓ	**46** Ⓕ Ⓖ Ⓗ Ⓙ
4 Ⓕ Ⓖ Ⓗ Ⓙ	**14** Ⓕ Ⓖ Ⓗ Ⓙ	**25** Ⓐ Ⓑ Ⓒ Ⓓ	**36** Ⓕ Ⓖ Ⓗ Ⓙ	**47** Ⓐ Ⓑ Ⓒ Ⓓ
5 Ⓐ Ⓑ Ⓒ Ⓓ	**15** Ⓐ Ⓑ Ⓒ Ⓓ	**26** Ⓕ Ⓖ Ⓗ Ⓙ	**37** Ⓐ Ⓑ Ⓒ Ⓓ	**48** Ⓕ Ⓖ Ⓗ Ⓙ
6 Ⓕ Ⓖ Ⓗ Ⓙ	**16** Ⓕ Ⓖ Ⓗ Ⓙ	**27** Ⓐ Ⓑ Ⓒ Ⓓ	**38** Ⓕ Ⓖ Ⓗ Ⓙ	**49** Ⓐ Ⓑ Ⓒ Ⓓ
7 Ⓐ Ⓑ Ⓒ Ⓓ	**17** Ⓐ Ⓑ Ⓒ Ⓓ Ⓔ	**28** Ⓕ Ⓖ Ⓗ Ⓙ	**39** Ⓐ Ⓑ Ⓒ Ⓓ	**50** Ⓕ Ⓖ Ⓗ Ⓙ
8 Ⓕ Ⓖ Ⓗ Ⓙ	**18** Ⓕ Ⓖ Ⓗ Ⓙ Ⓚ	**29** Ⓐ Ⓑ Ⓒ Ⓓ	**40** Ⓕ Ⓖ Ⓗ Ⓙ	**51** Ⓐ Ⓑ Ⓒ Ⓓ
9 Ⓐ Ⓑ Ⓒ Ⓓ	**19** Ⓐ Ⓑ Ⓒ Ⓓ Ⓔ	**30** Ⓕ Ⓖ Ⓗ Ⓙ	**41** Ⓐ Ⓑ Ⓒ Ⓓ	
10 Ⓕ Ⓖ Ⓗ Ⓙ	**20** Ⓕ Ⓖ Ⓗ Ⓙ Ⓚ	**31** Ⓐ Ⓑ Ⓒ Ⓓ	**42** Ⓕ Ⓖ Ⓗ Ⓙ	

Final Test Answer Sheet

Unit 3: Mathematics, pages 140–148

A Ⓐ Ⓑ Ⓒ Ⓓ Ⓔ	8 Ⓕ Ⓖ Ⓗ Ⓙ	18 Ⓕ Ⓖ Ⓗ Ⓙ	28 Ⓕ Ⓖ Ⓗ Ⓙ	38 Ⓕ Ⓖ Ⓗ Ⓙ
B Ⓕ Ⓖ Ⓗ Ⓙ Ⓚ	9 Ⓐ Ⓑ Ⓒ Ⓓ	19 Ⓐ Ⓑ Ⓒ Ⓓ	29 Ⓐ Ⓑ Ⓒ Ⓓ	39 Ⓐ Ⓑ Ⓒ Ⓓ
1 Ⓐ Ⓑ Ⓒ Ⓓ Ⓔ	10 Ⓕ Ⓖ Ⓗ Ⓙ	20 Ⓕ Ⓖ Ⓗ Ⓙ	30 Ⓕ Ⓖ Ⓗ Ⓙ	40 Ⓕ Ⓖ Ⓗ Ⓙ
2 Ⓕ Ⓖ Ⓗ Ⓙ Ⓚ	11 Ⓐ Ⓑ Ⓒ Ⓓ	21 Ⓐ Ⓑ Ⓒ Ⓓ	31 Ⓐ Ⓑ Ⓒ Ⓓ	41 Ⓐ Ⓑ Ⓒ Ⓓ
3 Ⓐ Ⓑ Ⓒ Ⓓ Ⓔ	12 Ⓕ Ⓖ Ⓗ Ⓙ	22 Ⓕ Ⓖ Ⓗ Ⓙ	32 Ⓕ Ⓖ Ⓗ Ⓙ	42 Ⓕ Ⓖ Ⓗ Ⓙ
4 Ⓕ Ⓖ Ⓗ Ⓙ Ⓚ	13 Ⓐ Ⓑ Ⓒ Ⓓ	23 Ⓐ Ⓑ Ⓒ Ⓓ	33 Ⓐ Ⓑ Ⓒ Ⓓ	43 Ⓐ Ⓑ Ⓒ Ⓓ
5 Ⓐ Ⓑ Ⓒ Ⓓ Ⓔ	14 Ⓕ Ⓖ Ⓗ Ⓙ	24 Ⓕ Ⓖ Ⓗ Ⓙ	34 Ⓕ Ⓖ Ⓗ Ⓙ	44 Ⓕ Ⓖ Ⓗ Ⓙ
6 Ⓕ Ⓖ Ⓗ Ⓙ Ⓚ	15 Ⓐ Ⓑ Ⓒ Ⓓ	25 Ⓐ Ⓑ Ⓒ Ⓓ	35 Ⓐ Ⓑ Ⓒ Ⓓ	45 Ⓐ Ⓑ Ⓒ Ⓓ
C Ⓐ Ⓑ Ⓒ Ⓓ	16 Ⓕ Ⓖ Ⓗ Ⓙ	26 Ⓕ Ⓖ Ⓗ Ⓙ	36 Ⓕ Ⓖ Ⓗ Ⓙ	
7 Ⓐ Ⓑ Ⓒ Ⓓ	17 Ⓐ Ⓑ Ⓒ Ⓓ	27 Ⓐ Ⓑ Ⓒ Ⓓ	37 Ⓐ Ⓑ Ⓒ Ⓓ	

Unit 4: Social Studies, pages 149–150

1 Ⓐ Ⓑ Ⓒ Ⓓ	4 Ⓕ Ⓖ Ⓗ Ⓙ	7 Ⓐ Ⓑ Ⓒ Ⓓ	10 Ⓕ Ⓖ Ⓗ Ⓙ
2 Ⓕ Ⓖ Ⓗ Ⓙ	5 Ⓐ Ⓑ Ⓒ Ⓓ	8 Ⓕ Ⓖ Ⓗ Ⓙ	11 Ⓐ Ⓑ Ⓒ Ⓓ
3 Ⓐ Ⓑ Ⓒ Ⓓ	6 Ⓕ Ⓖ Ⓗ Ⓙ	9 Ⓐ Ⓑ Ⓒ Ⓓ	

Unit 5: Science, pages 151–152

1 Ⓐ Ⓑ Ⓒ Ⓓ	4 Ⓕ Ⓖ Ⓗ Ⓙ	7 Ⓐ Ⓑ Ⓒ Ⓓ	10 Ⓕ Ⓖ Ⓗ Ⓙ	13 Ⓐ Ⓑ Ⓒ Ⓓ
2 Ⓕ Ⓖ Ⓗ Ⓙ	5 Ⓐ Ⓑ Ⓒ Ⓓ	8 Ⓕ Ⓖ Ⓗ Ⓙ	11 Ⓐ Ⓑ Ⓒ Ⓓ	
3 Ⓐ Ⓑ Ⓒ Ⓓ	6 Ⓕ Ⓖ Ⓗ Ⓙ	9 Ⓐ Ⓑ Ⓒ Ⓓ	12 Ⓕ Ⓖ Ⓗ Ⓙ	

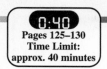

Pages 125–130
Time Limit:
approx. 40 minutes

Reading

Final Test
Reading

SAMPLE A

Frank was impatient waiting in the long movie line, but there was nothing he could do. It was a popular movie, and he wanted to see it on the first weekend it was playing. He probably

A has no idea what the movie will cost.

B doesn't know what the movie is about.

C expected the long line.

D enjoys waiting in line.

Directions: This story is about some young people who saw a problem and solved it. Read the story, then do numbers 1–4.

Dear Mr. Gallegos,

Last year, you taught our class about pollution and helped us plan a campus cleanup project. Something happened this summer that I think you will want to hear about.

My brother, Donovan, and I decided to have our own Park Cleanup Project. We followed the steps you taught us. First we outlined our goals and our time line. Then we asked our friends and parents to get involved. Each person signed up to do a job, like bringing trash bags, collecting trash, fixing things, or making signs. We posted signs at the park and handed out flyers.

The night before the cleanup day, I got a phone call. It was the mayor, Mrs. Lee, calling to tell me that she had heard about our project. She asked me to explain it to her. Mrs. Lee sounded like a nice lady, but I was afraid I was in trouble for planning the project without her permission. I swallowed my fear and told her all about it. There was a pause after I finished, but then she thanked me for getting involved and asked what time she should report for duty. Boy, was I relieved!

The next day, our group, including the mayor, spent all morning cleaning the park. When we were done Mrs. Lee told Donovan and me that we had made a big difference. She asked if we would help plan other cleanup projects.

I thought you would like to hear about this, because you were really the one who gave us the idea. Thanks a lot for your help.

Sincerely,
Jade King

GO

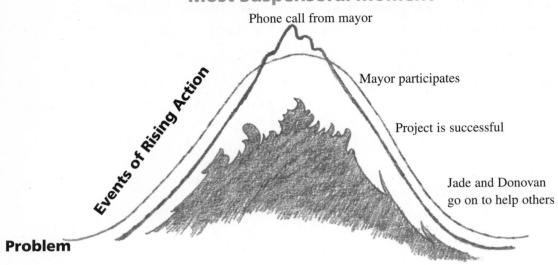

Most Suspenseful Moment

Phone call from mayor

Mayor participates

Project is successful

Jade and Donovan
go on to help others

Events of Rising Action

Problem

1 **Which of these belongs in the area marked "Events of Rising Action"?**

A Jade and Donovan help other people plan cleanup projects.

B The mayor brings some city maintenance workers to help.

C Jade and her friends publicize and plan the cleanup day.

D Some people bring trash bags and others pick up trash.

2 **Choose the picture that shows what would best fit in the area labeled "Problem."**

F   **G**   **H**   **J**

3 **What has Jade learned about herself by the end of the passage?**

A Sometimes the things you learn in school aren't very useful.

B Great changes can begin with just one or two people.

C If you volunteer for work you will just be asked to do more.

D She is better than anyone else at thinking of good ideas.

GO

4   **How will Jade probably be different as a result of this experience?**

  F   She will no longer litter on public property.

  G   She will try to work more cooperatively with her brother.

  H   She will pay closer attention in the classroom.

  J   She will be even more active in her community.

Directions: Here is part of a student report about noise pollution.
There are some mistakes that need correcting.

¹ There are many different kinds of pollution, but can you think of one you can actually hear? ² Noise pollution is caused by loud sounds made by cars, airplanes, or trains. ³ It can also come from lawnmowers and stereos. ⁴ Cities are much noisier than other areas. ⁵ Researchers believe that noise increases stress and decreases health. ⁶ Most people simply gets used to the level of noise in their environment.

5   **Which is the best way to write Sentence 6?**

  A   Most people simply get used to the level of noise in their environment.

  B   Most people were simply getting used to the level of noise in their environment.

  C   Most people simply got used to the level of noise in their environment.

  D   Best as it is

6   **Which sentence would best follow Sentence 4?**

  F   Noise pollution is invisible because it cannot be seen; it can only be heard.

  G   Because of this, people in big cities are more likely to suffer the effects of noise pollution.

  H   There are many things that contribute to the levels of noise in our lives.

  J   Most kinds of pollution, like air and water pollution, are visible.

GO

Directions: This is an application for a summer music and dance workshop. Use the application to do numbers 7–9.

Junior Regional Music and Dance Workshop Application

Complete one application for each participant.
Return completed application to the office by January 30.
The workshop itself is free, but be sure to enclose a check
for $10 if you plan to eat lunch with the group.

Upon acceptance of your application, you will receive in
the mail a confirmation of your participation, a lunch voucher,
and a schedule.

Name of student: _____

Parent/Guardian: _____

Street address: _____

Home phone: _____ **Work phone:** _____

Student's grade   6   7   8

School student attends: _____

Activities you plan to attend:

Morning sessions: (circle 2)

beginning jazz band   intermediate ballet

intermediate choir   beginning tap dance

orchestra (all levels)   beginning jazz dance

Afternoon sessions: (circle 2)

marching band   beginning folk dance

intermediate tap dance   beginning choir

beginning guitar   beginning ballet

---

7 **What do applicants get to do if they pay ten dollars?**

A eat lunch with the group

B learn some new dances

C learn new songs to play

D find out the schedule

8 **Which of these activities is not offered at the workshop?**

F beginning tap dance

G intermediate ballet

H intermediate guitar

J beginning jazz band

9 **The word *voucher* probably refers to**

A a lunch sack filled with food.

B a ticket used to pay for lunch.

C a list of what people will eat.

D something very good to eat.

GO

Directions: Read the passage. Then answer the questions.

A Sports Superstar

Today, famous athletes can earn million-dollar salaries and live like movie stars. But not so long ago, things were very different. For Olympic runner Jesse Owens, being an athlete was not so glamorous.

Jesse Owens was born to a poor family in Alabama in 1913. The family soon moved to Ohio, where Jesse discovered that he loved to run.

Jesse attended Ohio State University, but being a track star didn't make life much easier for him. Ohio State was still segregated when Jesse entered in 1933. Black students like Jesse could not live on campus with white classmates. Jesse had to use "blacks-only" restaurants and hotels when he traveled with his team. But he continued to work hard and by the time he was a junior, Jesse had already broken three world's records!

Jesse was determined to make it to the Olympics. But there were people who didn't want him to go. That's because the 1936 Olympics were held in Berlin, a part of Nazi Germany. The Nazi leader, Adolph Hitler, thought the Berlin Olympics would prove that white athletes were better than all other athletes, including blacks.

When Jesse did compete in Berlin, he stunned everyone. He won four Gold Medals—in the 100-meter dash, the 200-meter dash, the broad jump, and 400-meter relay—more than any American track athlete had ever won at the Olympics! Jesse had proven that a person's success in life is determined by individual ability, not race.

Even after the triumph in Berlin, though, Jesse had to struggle. He still had to work a variety of jobs to support his family. He loved working with underprivileged kids like he had been. He became director of the Chicago Boys' Club.

Because of his hard work, President Eisenhower's administration named Jesse "Ambassador of Sports" and sent him to travel the world, talking to people from different countries about his experience as an Olympian. Jesse also won such high honors as the United States Medal of Freedom, the President's Living Legend Award, and the Congressional Gold Medal.

10 In this passage, what does *segregated* mean?

F people of different races were encouraged to live together

G people of different races were kept apart

H people of different races could eat in the same restaurants

J people of different races had to meet different academic requirements

11 What is one clue that tells you that Jesse was a hard worker?

A He broke three world's records and went to the Olympics.

B He won Gold Medals in the Olympics even though some people were against him.

C He became a runner even though his family was very poor.

D He struggled to support his family while he was in college and after the Olympics.

GO

Directions: Choose the best answer for each of the following.

12 **Respite is to rest as resignation is to**

   F sit

   G withdraw

   H intermission

   J nap

13 **Peanut is to legume as evergreen is to**

   A nut

   B butter

   C forest

   D conifer

14 **Synonyms are to thesaurus as statistics are to**

   F almanac

   G dictionary

   H atlas

   J numbers

15 **Millimeter is to ladybug as centimeter is to**

   A elephant

   B plant cell

   C sparrow

   D ant

Directions: Match words with the **same** meanings.

16	strengthen	**F**	impulsive
17	severe	**G**	dizzy
18	reeling	**H**	drastic
19	impetuous	**J**	intensify

Directions: Match words with **opposite** meanings.

20	criticize	**A**	persist
21	falter	**B**	expose
22	allow	**C**	extol
23	veil	**D**	prohibit

24	punctual	**F**	incompetent
25	capable	**G**	unqualified
26	eligible	**H**	concealed
27	visible	**J**	tardy

STOP

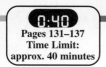

0:40
Pages 131–137
Time Limit:
approx. 40 minutes

Language Arts

Final Test
Language Arts

UNIT **2**

Directions: For Sample A and numbers 1 and 2, read the sentences. Choose the word that correctly completes **both** sentences.

> **SAMPLE A**
>
> All workers _____ to Mr. Lee.
>
> I did a _____ on earthquakes.
>
> **A** answer **C** report
> **B** project **D** respond

1 The _____ carried grain to Africa.
A glass _____ held the medication.

A ship **C** craft
B container **D** vessel

2 The service _____ was ten dollars.
I have to _____ this battery.

F fee **H** charge
G energize **J** cost

Directions: For numbers 3 and 4, choose the word that means the **opposite** of the underlined word.

3 apathetic group

A listless **C** realistic
B enthusiastic **D** enlightened

4 rash decision

F thoughtful **H** momentous
G impetuous **J** timely

Directions: For numbers 5 and 6, read the paragraph. For each numbered blank, there is a list of words with the same number. Choose the word from each list that best completes the meaning of the paragraph.

When her parents had decided that they should take a two-week vacation together and ride around the country by bus, Marsha was __(5)__. However, the trip turned out to be really fun. She knew she would be __(6)__ when the journey came to an end.

5 **A** confident
B reluctant
C impatient
D ecstatic

6 **F** dismayed
G unlikely
H disinterested
J disarrayed

GO

Directions: For numbers 7 and 8, choose the answer that is written correctly and shows the correct capitalization and punctuation.

7 **A** "How old are these picture books, asked Elliot?"

  B Sebastian asked, "What kind of books do you sell?"

  C Ravi said "that is a used book-store across the street."

  D Hal said, "be careful, some of these books are fragile."

8 **F** He ordered tomato soup and a turkey burger, his favorite lunch.

  G Mrs. O'Malley the owner, greeted the diners as they walked in.

  H The honey mustard dressing, made without fat is very popular.

  J On special occasions we order filet mignon the chef's specialty.

Directions: For numbers 9–12, look at the underlined part of the paragraph. Choose the answer that shows the best capitalization and punctuation for that part.

(9)   A strange thing happened at the Restaurant last night. We
(10)   walked in and the head waiter announced, "You are the 10,000th
(11)   patron your meal is free." When we sat down, everyone made a
(12)   big fuss. The food was wonderful; and we had a great time.

9 **A** restaurant. Last
  B Restaurant Last
  C restaurant last
  D Correct as it is

11 **A** patron. Your
  B patron: your
  C Patron your
  D Correct as it is

10 **F** announced "You
  G announced, you
  H announced. You
  J Correct as it is

12 **F** wonderful. And
  G wonderful, and
  H wonderful? And
  J Correct as it is

GO

Directions: For Sample B and numbers 13–16, choose the word that is spelled correctly and best completes the sentence.

SAMPLE
B
The new business was _____.

A sucessful   C successful
B succesful   D successfull

13 This _____ is really funny.

A comercial
B commersial
C commerciel
D commercial

14 Hand me the _____ wrench.

F adjustable
G ajustable
H adjustible
J adjustabel

15 She was the county _____.

A administrater
B addministrator
C administrator
D adminustrator

16 They studied English _____.

F litrature
G literature
H literachur
J litterature

Directions: For numbers 17–20, read each phrase. Find the underlined word that is **not** spelled correctly. If all the underlined words are spelled correctly, mark "All correct."

17 A erroneous idea
B cause interference
C good justification
D make restitution
E All correct

18 F dynamic personality
G huge alligater
H apparel store
J feel ecstatic
K All correct

19 A correct grammer
B science laboratory
C occasionally late
D voluntary job
E All correct

20 F with gratitude
G artificial flowers
H believable impostor
J abstract problem
K All correct

GO

Directions: For numbers 21–32, find the choice that is spelled correctly.

21
- **A** photosinthesis
- **B** photosyntheses
- **C** photosynthesis
- **D** photocynthesis

22
- **F** lusious
- **G** luscous
- **H** lusciouis
- **J** luscious

23
- **A** entrepreneur
- **B** entrepenour
- **C** entreprenour
- **D** entrepenore

24
- **F** inevitible
- **G** inevitable
- **H** inevetible
- **J** inevetable

25
- **A** leuge
- **B** leage
- **C** legue
- **D** league

26
- **F** insuffishent
- **G** insufficent
- **H** insuficient
- **J** insufficient

27
- **A** spirituol
- **B** spiritual
- **C** spirituel
- **D** spiritoul

28
- **F** anonimus
- **G** anonymus
- **H** anonymous
- **J** anonimous

29
- **A** apologize
- **B** apoligize
- **C** appologize
- **D** apolagize

30
- **F** satillite
- **G** satelitte
- **H** satelite
- **J** satellite

31
- **A** perenniel
- **B** prennial
- **C** perennial
- **D** perenial

32
- **F** vacinate
- **G** vaccinate
- **H** vaccinnate
- **J** vaccanate

GO

Directions: For questions 33–40, mark the answer that shows how the underlined word or phrase should be written correctly.

33 They immediately returned the bike to <u>him and I.</u>

   A he and me.

   B he and I

   C him and me.

   D Correct as is

34 Mrs. Lapidus asked <u>who book was</u> on the table.

   F whose book was

   G who's book was

   H whose was the book

   J Correct as is

35 After <u>we did eliminated</u> everyone else, we were able to identify the culprit.

   A we had eliminated

   B we were eliminating

   C we were eliminated

   D Correct as is

36 "I never <u>seen nothing funnier than that there movie,</u>" Flip announced.

   F saw nothing funnier than that

   G seen anything funnier than that there

   H saw anything funnier than that

   J Correct as it is

37 No one loves animals <u>more than me!</u>

   A more than I!

   B more then me!

   C more then I!

   D Correct as is

38 <u>"To whom are you speaking?"</u> she asked.

   F "To who are you speaking?"

   G "Who are you speaking?"

   H "Who is you speaking to?"

   J Correct as is

39 <u>Tanya and me</u> went to the zoo.

   A Tanya and I

   B Us

   C Tanya and myself

   D Correct as is

40 I need a dress for my only <u>sisters</u> wedding.

   F sisters's

   G sisters'

   H sister's

   J Correct as is

GO

Directions: For numbers 41–44, find the word or phrase that correctly completes each sentence.

41 She built that porch _____.

   A theirselves
   B herself
   C themselves
   D himself

42 If Maxwell hadn't taken Fluffer to the vet, she _____ really sick.

   F could have got
   G could have gotten
   H will have got
   J will have gotten

43 There _____ no good explanation for what happened in the auditorium.

   A ain't
   B isn't
   C is
   D is not

44 _____ the largest statue in the world.

   F It be
   G Its
   H It's
   J Its'

Directions: For numbers 45 and 46, find the choice that best combines the sentences.

45 Theresa is a great soccer player. Theresa is a great tennis player. Theresa really has a hard time with basketball.

   A Theresa is a great soccer player and a great tennis player; but she really has a hard time with basketball.
   B Theresa is a great soccer player; she is a great tennis player; but she has a hard time with basketball.
   C Theresa is a great soccer and tennis player, but she really has a hard time with basketball.
   D Theresa is a great soccer player and tennis player but she really has a hard time with basketball.

46 The ball flew up into the air. The crowd stopped. It was a homerun!

   F When the ball flew up into the air, the crowd stopped, it was a homerun!
   G When the ball flew up into the air; the crowd stopped, it was a homerun!
   H When the ball flew up into the air, the crowd stopped; it was a homerun!
   J When the ball flew up into the air the crowd stopped, it was a homerun!

GO

Directions: For numbers 47–49, choose the sentence that shows correct punctuation and capitalization.

47 **A** Havent you finished yet?

B Youll have to clean your room this afternoon.

C They did n't expect their guests to arrive that early.

D Kadri doesn't know his cousin has already arrived.

48 **F** Go right on Lomas street and continue for a few blocks.

G The San Diego Zoo, is famous around the world.

H The Ocean was too rough for us to swim.

J Visiting a foreign country is a wonderful experience.

49 **A** Mark Twain wrote for the new york tribune.

B Have you read The Legend of Sleepy Hollow?

C What is your favorite book.

D I just finished the first Chapter today.

Directions: Read the following paragraph and answer questions 50 and 51.

A surprising number of people like to assemble their own furniture. They buy kits that contain everything needed, from wood to screws. Furniture kits can be purchased from mail-order houses or walk-in retailers. These kits are less expensive than regular furniture, yet the quality of the finished product is high. In addition, assembling a kit gives someone a sense of accomplishment.

50 **Choose the best concluding sentence to add to this paragraph.**

F Traditional furniture comes assembled from the factory.

G People decorate their houses with different styles of furniture.

H Because of these advantages, more and more people are buying furniture kits.

J Many other products are also bought through mail order.

51 **What is the best way to write the underlined part of sentence 3?**

A will be purchased

B are purchasing

C to be purchased

D Correct as is

STOP

Directions: Write a paper describing one of your closest friends in detail.

_____

_____

_____

_____

_____

_____

_____

_____

_____

_____

_____

_____

_____

_____

_____

_____

_____

_____

_____

_____

GO

Directions: Write an essay comparing two of your favorite authors.

_____

_____

_____

_____

_____

_____

_____

_____

_____

_____

_____

_____

_____

_____

_____

_____

_____

_____

_____

_____

_____

STOP

Mathematics

SAMPLE A

$8 (6 - 2) =$

A 46
B 50
C 32
D 44
E None of these

SAMPLE B

$40 + {}^-25 =$

F $^-65$
G $^-15$
H 65
J 25
K None of these

1

$^-50 \times {}^-6 =$

A $^-300$
B 300
C $^-56$
D 56
E None of these

4

$$9\tfrac{5}{6}$$
$$- \tfrac{7}{12}$$

F $9\tfrac{1}{6}$
G $8\tfrac{1}{4}$
H $9\tfrac{1}{3}$
J $9\tfrac{1}{2}$
K None of these

2

$$2\tfrac{2}{3}$$
$$+ 4\tfrac{5}{8}$$

F 7
G $7\tfrac{7}{24}$
H $7\tfrac{5}{8}$
J $6\tfrac{7}{24}$
K None of these

5

30% of ☐ = 24

A 21
B 72
C 80
D 720
E None of these

3

$0.042 \div 6 =$

A 0.7
B 0.07
C 0.007
D 0.0007
E None of these

6

$.039 \times 7 =$

F 2.73
G 0.273
H 0.0273
J 0.00273
K None of these

GO

SAMPLE C

What are all the common factors of 22 and 44?

A 1, 2, 11, and 22
B 1 and 22
C 1, 2, 11, 22, 44, and 88
D 1, 2, 11, 22, and 44

---

7 If these percents were converted to decimals, which one would fall between Point X and Point Y on the number line?

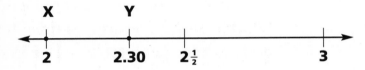

A 175%
B 215%
C 240%
D 257%

---

8 If this pattern continues, how many squares will there be in Figure 5?

F 30
G 20
H 18
J 36

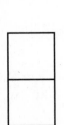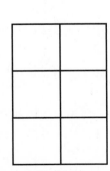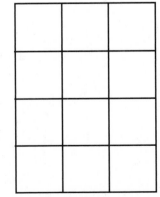

Figure 1   **Figure 2**   **Figure 3**   **Figure 4**   **Figure 5**

GO

Directions: Juanita is going to buy a computer. She has been given the opinions of 4 friends, who already have computers, on which brand she should buy. Each brand has a different price and different features such as additional memory, increased processor speed, fax modem, and CD-ROM. Think about this when you do numbers 9 and 10.

9 Juanita wants to spend between $1250 and $1500 on a new computer. According to the graph, which computer should she buy?

Price Comparison

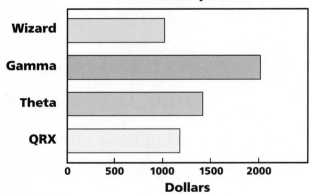

A Wizard
B Gamma
C Theta
D QRX

10 The graph shows the number of features that each computer has. Tetsuo wants to buy a computer that has many features, and he does not want to spend too much money. What should he look for on the graphs?

Features

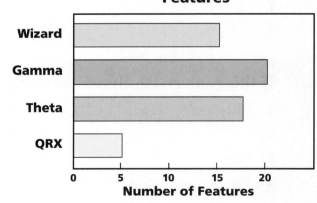

F a computer with a short bar on both graphs

G a computer with a long bar on both graphs

H a computer with a short bar on the features graph and a long bar on the price graph

J a computer with a long bar on the features graph and a short bar on the price graph

GO

SCHOOL SNACK BAR

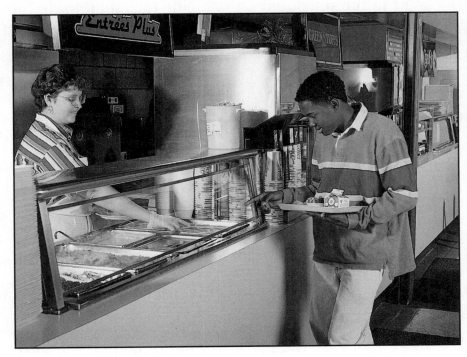

Directions: The new snack bar at the Ridge Street School has just opened. Think about this when you do numbers 11–15.

11 **The two soft drink bottles are**

- **A** neither congruent nor similar.
- **B** congruent but not similar.
- **C** similar but not congruent.
- **D** similar and congruent.

12 **Which of these sampling methods will give the best random sample of 65 students from the entire school population of 650?**

- **F** Choose the 65 students in Mr. Green's advanced computer classes.
- **G** Select the first 65 students that walk out the front door of the school at the end of the day.
- **H** Choose the 65 students with the highest grade point averages.
- **J** Select the 65 oldest children at the school.

GO

13 The table shows the number of students who went to the snack bar after school on the first four days that it was open.

Day	Number of Students
1	78
2	89
3	101
4	114
5	

If the pattern continues, how many students will go to the snack bar after school on Day 5?

A 125

B 126

C 127

D 128

14 The snack bar is 24 feet long and 18 feet wide. If it were $\frac{1}{3}$ the length and 3 times the width, how would its area change?

F It would increase by 24 square feet.

G It would decrease by 30 square feet.

H It would be three times as large.

J It would remain the same.

15 The picture shows the cards that the fans hold up to form a red "R" for Ridge Street School every time the football team scores. About what percent of the cards as a whole are red?

A 10%

B 30%

C 50%

D 70%

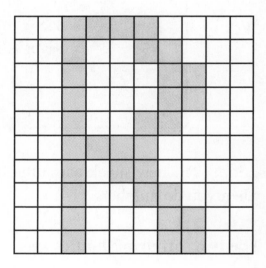

GO

Directions: Mark the letter next to the correct answer for numbers 16–25.

16

$10 \div \frac{1}{5} =$

F   2
G $2\frac{1}{5}$
H   50
J   None of these

17

$0.7\overline{)1.61}$

A   2.3
B   20.3
C   0.171
D   None of these

18

$(12 - 9) \times 7 =$

F   ⁻51
G   21
H   4
J   None of these

19

30% of 8 =

A   2.4
B   3.8
C   8.3
D   8.03

20

$700 \div {}^{-}35 =$

F   ⁻665
G   6655
H   ⁻20
J   735

21

$5^{2} - (8 \times 3) =$

A   1
B   51
C   14
D   20

22

$69.2 \times 4.6 =$

F   3.1832
G   31.832
H   318.32
J   3183.2

23

$^{-}20 \times 8 =$

A   160
B   ⁻160
C   28
D   ⁻28

24

G $5\frac{1}{8}$
$- 2\frac{2}{3}$

F $6\frac{3}{5}$
  $3\frac{1}{5}$
H $3\frac{11}{24}$
J $2\frac{11}{24}$

25

$2 \div \frac{2}{3} =$

A   3
B $\frac{1}{3}$
C $1\frac{1}{3}$
D $2\frac{2}{3}$

GO

Directions: Mark the letter next to the correct answer for numbers 26–33.

26 **What is the greatest common factor of 27, 36, and 54?**

F 3
G 0
H 9
J 18

27 **Which of these is the reciprocal of $\frac{8}{7}$?**

A $\frac{1}{7}$
B 8
C $\frac{1}{8}$
D $\frac{7}{8}$

28 **For which of these equations would $a = 5$ when $b = 6$?**

F $a - b = 11$
G $a + b = 11$
H $a + b = 1$
J $a - b = 1$

29 **Which of these is another way to write 3^5?**

A 3×5
B $3 \times 3 \times 3 \times 3 \times 3$
C $3 + 3 + 3 + 3 + 3$
D 53

30 **Which of these fractions is closest to 0?**

F $\frac{1}{4}$
G $\frac{2}{12}$
H $\frac{1}{6}$
J $\frac{1}{9}$

31 **The closest estimate of $4\frac{9}{10} \times 5\frac{6}{7}$ is**

A 20
B 25
C 30
D 36

32 **$[(5 \times 5) + 3] \div 4 + 10 =$**

F 7
G 17
H 20
J 10

33 **For which of these equations would $x = 6$ when $y = 12$?**

A $x = 3y$
B $x = 2y$
C $x = \frac{1}{2}y$
D $x = \frac{1}{3}y$

GO

Directions: Choose the correct answer for numbers 34–39.

34 A sporting goods store is having a sale on T-shirts. If you buy one T-shirt at regular price, you can buy the second T-shirt at half price. If the regular price of one T-shirt is $11, how much would it cost to buy two?

   F $11

   G $22

   H $16.50

   J Not enough information

35 There are different time zones in the United States. When it is 9:00 P.M. in New York, it is 6:00 P.M. in California. If a plane leaves New York at 8:00 A.M. New York time and lands in California at 11:00 A.M. California time, how long was the flight?

   A 2 hours

   B 6 hours

   C 7 hours

   D 8 hours

36 In triangle ABC, angle A measures 45 degrees. Angle B measures 7 degrees more than angle C. What is the measure of angle C?

   F 45 degrees

   G 71 degrees

   H 64 degrees

   J Not enough information

37 Which group of integers is in order from greatest to least?

   A 10, 3, 0, $^-$1, $^-$10

   B 10, 3, 0, $^-$10, 1

   C $^-$1, $^-$10, 0, 3, 10

   D $^-$10, $^-$1, 0, 3, 10

38 $57 + {}^-101 =$

   F $^-$158

   G 158

   H $^-$44

   J 1936

39 What is the square root of 289?

   A 11

   B 13

   C 17

   D 19

GO

Directions: Choose the correct answer for numbers 40–45.

40 Pamela has a trunk that is
1.1 meters long, 0.4 meters high,
and .7 meters wide. What is the
volume of the trunk?

F 0.308 cubic meters

G 2.2 cubic meters

H 30.8 cubic meters

J 4.4 cubic meters

41 Jameela arrived at the museum at
2:30. Michael arrived 1 hour and
ten minutes later. Alana arrived
25 minutes after Michael. At what
time did Alana arrive?

A 2:55

B 3:40

C 4:05

D None of the above

42 Two numbers have a product of
446,880, and their sum, when
divided in half, equals 686. What
are the numbers?

F 562 and 810

G 532 and 840

H 446 and 926

J Not enough information

43 A triangle measures 0.75 meters
high and 0.4 meters wide at its base.
What is the area of the triangle?

A 3 square meters

B 0.3 square meters

C 1.5 square meters

D 0.15 square meters

44 Carmella is holding a bake sale for
charity. She will sell pies at a price
of $12 each, 75% of which she will
give to the charity. If she sells
32 pies altogether, how much will
she money will she raise for the
charity?

F $384

G $288

H $24

J Not enough information

45 Which is the correct answer to
$7 + 5 \times 3 - 8 \div 2$?

A 18

B 14

C 6

D 20

STOP

Pages 149–150
Time Limit:
approx. 15 minutes

Final Test
Social Studies

UNIT 4

Social Studies

Directions: Study the time line that shows important events in the development of transportation in the United States. Then do numbers 1–5.

Transportation in the United States

Robert Fulton's steam-powered boat, the *Clermont*, makes a round trip between Albany and New York in five days.

More than 30,000 miles of railroad track connect towns across the U.S.

The first refrigerator cars are used to keep produce fresh during transport.

The first successful turnpike (tollroad) opens.

The United States has developed more than 3,000 miles of canals and 3,000 miles of railroad track.

The Erie Canal is completed.

Illinois passes the first "Granger" law to regulate railroads.

Autos powered by gasoline are invented.

1794   1807   1825   1840   1860   1869   1870's   1892

---

1 How many years passed between the time the U.S. developed 3,000 miles of railroad track and 30,000 miles of railroad track?

A 10 years
B 2 decades
C half of a century
D These events happened during the same year.

2 When did Illinois pass the first Granger law?

F after the *Clermont* sailed
G before the Erie Canal was completed
H during the eighteenth century
J at the same time as refrigerator cars rolled across the country

3 During which year is a transportation milestone not related to land travel listed?

A 1794   C 1860
B 1825   D 1869

4 How many years after 3,000 miles of track had been laid did Illinois pass a law to regulate railroads?

F 9 years   H 49 years
G 29 years   J 59 years

5 Which happened earliest?

A Autos chugged across the country.
B Illinois passed a law to regulate railroads.
C Robert Fulton's boat sailed.
D The U.S. laid more than 3,000 miles of railroad track.

GO

Directions: For numbers 6–11, choose the correct answer.

6 **Which President sent Meriwether Lewis and William Clark on an expedition to explore the West?**

F George Washington

G John Tyler

H Thomas Jefferson

J Ulysses S. Grant

7 **How did Thomas Jefferson and James Madison try to change British action prior to 1812?**

A through strong military force

B through economic sanctions

C through writing letters and sending official documents

D through a laissez-faire policy

8 **Which was a major cause of the War of 1812?**

F glutting the market with foreign goods

G enacting railroad strikes

H interfering with sailing routes

J placing an embargo on crops

9 **Which of the following was not a major result of the Industrial Revolution in the United States?**

A electricity

B completion of modern transportation and communication systems

C westward expansion

D application of science to industrial workings and new products

10 **Who opposed declaration of war in the War of 1812?**

F farmers

G Thomas Jefferson

H James Madison

J New Englanders

11 **Who among the following is not associated with the American Industrial Revolution?**

A Bette Nesmith Graham and liquid paper

B Eli Whiney and the cotton gin

C Alexander Graham Bell and the telephone

D Thomas Edison and the electric lamp

STOP

Science

Directions: For numbers 1–8, choose the correct answer.

1 A positively charged particle, found within the nucleus of an atom, is called

   A a proton.

   B a neutron.

   C an electron.

   D a chloroplast.

2 The chemical symbol for steam is

   F HO_2

   G HO

   H H_2O

   J O_2H

3 To measure the amount of gas produced by a chemical reaction, the most exact method to use would be

   A observation.

   B barometric pressure.

   C heating and cooling it.

   D water displacement.

4 Which of the following is not one of the states of matter?

   F gas

   G compound

   H solid

   J liquid

5 The temperature at which, when heated, a substance changes from solid to liquid is called its

   A boiling point.

   B freezing point.

   C liquefying point.

   D melting point.

6 What is the term for a piece of a meteor that reaches the Earth's surface before burning up?

   F a meteorite

   G an asteroid

   H a comet

   J a UFO

7 H is the symbol of what element?

   A helium

   B holmium

   C hafnium

   D hydrogen

8 Which planet is smallest and coldest?

   F Jupiter

   G Pluto

   H Earth

   J Venus

GO

Directions: The following graph shows the population growth of two different species of birds in the Lumalona nature preserve over a century. Study the graph carefully, then use it to answer numbers 9–13.

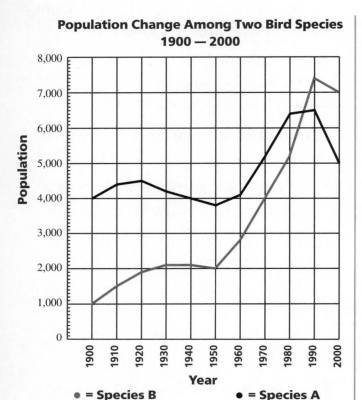

Population Change Among Two Bird Species 1900 — 2000

● = Species B   ● = Species A

9 **What type of graph is shown here?**

A   a simple bar graph

B   a double line graph

C   a simple line graph

D   a triple line graph

10 **Which species had a higher population in 1900?**

F   species A

G   species B

H   the populations were the same

J   Not enough information

11 **Which species had a higher population in 1990?**

A   species A

B   species B

C   the populations were the same

D   Not enough information

12 **Around what year did the population of species B surpass the population of species A?**

F   1980   H   1990

G   1985   J   1995

13 **Based on this graph alone, what is one possible explanation for the decrease in both populations in the 1990's?**

A   There was a large-scale migration of birds out of the area due to changes in the climate.

B   A conflict arose between the two species when the population of species B grew dramatically.

C   There was a massive environmental disaster which instantly threatened both populations with extinction.

D   The surge in both populations caused a drain on natural resources the birds depended on, causing a gradual adjustment in both populations.

STOP

NOTES

NOTES